Getting It Right

Other Titles of Interest
by Raymond L. Calabrese

The Dissertation Desk Reference

The Doctoral Student's Manual to Writing the Dissertation

The Doctoral Student's Advisor and Mentor: Sage Advice from the Experts

*The Faculty Mentor's Wisdom: Conceptualizing, Writing,
and Defending the Dissertation*

Getting It Right

The Essential Elements of a Dissertation

New Edition

Raymond L. Calabrese

ROWMAN & LITTLEFIELD EDUCATION
A division of
ROWMAN & LITTLEFIELD PUBLISHERS, INC.
Lanham • New York • Toronto • Plymouth, UK

Published by Rowman & Littlefield Education
A division of Rowman & Littlefield Publishers, Inc.
A wholly owned subsidiary of The Rowman & Littlefield Publishing Group, Inc.
4501 Forbes Boulevard, Suite 200, Lanham, Maryland 20706
www.rowman.com

10 Thornbury Road, Plymouth PL6 7PP, United Kingdom

British Library Cataloguing in Publication Information Available

Library of Congress Cataloging-in-Publication Data
Calabrese, Raymond L., 1942–
Getting it right : the essential elements of a dissertation / Raymond L. Calabrese.—New ed.
Rev. ed. of: The elements of an effective dissertation and thesis, c2006.
p. cm.
Includes bibliographical references.
ISBN 978-1-61048-920-1 (pbk. : alk. paper)—ISBN 978-1-61048-921-8 (electronic)
1. Dissertations, Academic. 2. Report writing. 3. Research. I. Calabrese, Raymond L., 1942– Elements of an effective dissertation and thesis. II. Title.
LB2369.C275 2012
808.06′6378—dc23
2012026760

☉™ The paper used in this publication meets the minimum requirements of American National Standard for Information Sciences Permanence of Paper for Printed Library Materials, ANSI/NISO Z39.48-1992.

Printed in the United States of America

Contents

Preface

Getting it Right: The Elements of a Dissertation is the second edition of *The Elements of an Effective Dissertation and Thesis*. The change in title reflects a commitment to provide the reader with a clearer understanding of the dissertation processes while providing significant upgrades for the reader. The following are a sample of the upgrades:

- A number of new and more contemporary examples of dissertations
- *Quick Tips* that provide the reader with instant mentoring advice
- A list of dissertation headers at the front of each chapter that serve as a chapter organizer for the reader
- A *pep talk* at the end of each chapter that provides motivation for the researcher to continue working on the dissertation toward a successful defense
- A motivational quotation at the end of each chapter to provide inspiration to remain focused
- Guidance and advice on how to choose an advisor and committee
- The second edition is written for the dissertation researcher. The familiar "you" is replaced with "the researcher"

WHY I WROTE THIS BOOK

I remember my struggles in writing my dissertation. I learned about endurance, patience, courage, and fortitude. I learned what to do and what not to do. I also believed there were clear examples I could use as a model in writing my dissertation. I discovered the examples in my review of the best dissertations in my field. The examples taught me how to organize my dissertation and how to effectively describe and report my study.

As a doctoral student advisor, I apply many of the lessons I learned. I want my doctoral students to move quickly beyond the tedious tasks associated with writing the dissertation and to be more passionately involved in the creative aspects of their work, which includes conducting their research and reporting the results of their research in the form of a dissertation designed to make a difference. I do this by providing them with salient examples of what should go in a quality dissertation. In this book, *Getting it Right: The Elements of a Dissertation,* I share the same advice with you, the reader.

I know that writing the dissertation is not easy. Staying focused, working hard, and learning to work with people to produce a quality product are important and often difficult parts of a successful dissertation. Success requires something more than working hard. It requires working smart. Consequently, I wrote this book to demystify and simplify the dissertation writing process. You have to do the work; however, following the map provided in this book will greatly facilitate the process.

HOW THIS BOOK WILL HELP YOU

Getting it Right: The Elements of a Dissertation provides you with a description, definition, and example of each dissertation element — think of the elements as headers or subheaders in each chapter. It is reader friendly. You will understand what belongs in the dissertation and where it belongs.

Getting it Right: The Elements of a Dissertation uses the traditional five-chapter dissertation as a basic model. Although I recognize the existence of multiple dissertation formats, I've found that alternative dissertation formats share similar components or elements with the traditional five-chapter model. As a result, you will find what you need to be successful in writing your dissertation.

The five-chapter format follows a pattern:

Chapter 1 — the introduction, statement of the problem, and research questions
Chapter 2 — a review of the relevant literature
Chapter 3 — the methodology used in the study
Chapter 4 — the presentation of results or findings
Chapter 5 — the discussion of the results or findings

Within each chapter of *Getting it Right: The Elements of a Dissertation*, you will find elements for that chapter. The elements in chapter 1, for example, include an introduction, background of the study, problem statement, purpose of the study, significance of the study, overview of methodology, research questions, research hypotheses, objectives/outcomes, limitations, delimitations, assumptions, definition of key terms, and organization of the dissertation. In each case, the *element* generally is associated with a header within the dissertation.

To facilitate the process of writing a dissertation, the table of contents and index are reader-friendly; you can look for guidance with a particular phase of the dissertation by consulting the index. If you need to see an example of a research question, you can go to the table of contents, look under chapter 1, and find the section for research questions, or refer to the index.

Getting it Right: The Elements of a Dissertation contains samples from more than one hundred completed dissertations from well-known universities and colleges. I quoted from dissertations not as exemplars, but as guides, indicating how these scholars completed their task and met the rigorous academic standards of their department and institution, leading to a successful completion. These samples are contained in the highlighted Examples sections of each chapter.

In reviewing an exhaustive array of dissertations I concluded no one standard format fits all. There is, however, general agreement as to the elements that comprise excellent research. In the end, you must take personal responsibility for conducting your research and writing your dissertation. *Getting it Right: The Elements of a Dissertation* provides the map and markers needed to complete a scholarly dissertation. Good luck.

Quick Tip: Choosing the right advisor and committee members leads to a successful defense and quality dissertation.

CHOOSING AN ADVISOR AND COMMITTEE

In this section I share the wisdom and lessons I learned in working with dissertation advisees. I have two primary goals for my advisees: (1) defend a high-quality dissertation, and (2) use the dissertation as a launching pad to make great accomplishments. I want the same for you. The following *work smart* comments will help you with important challenges in the dissertation process.

Choice of Advisor

I have three questions to consider when choosing an advisor:

- Does the advisor have time for you?
- What is the advisor's track record with other students?
- Does the advisor's expertise match your interests?

Three "yeses" are needed for a choice of advisor.

Selecting the Dissertation Committee

Membership on your dissertation committee is an opportunity for you to shape your doctoral experience. My advisees and I have a substantive conversation regarding membership. Here are the criteria I ask my advisees to use:

- Will the member "play well" with other members?
- Will the member contribute meaningfully to the study?
- Does the member have the potential to advance your career after the dissertation is completed?
- Is the member a mentor?

Four "yeses" are needed for membership on the dissertation committee.

Acknowledgments

Dr. Thomas F. Koerner, editorial director at Rowman & Littlefield Education, is a rare combination of a highly skilled and competent professional and an authentically genuine and good human being. Tom encourages, inspires, and motivates all associated with him to be better. His understanding of higher education made this project more pleasure than work for me.

Others at Rowman & Littlefield have also been supportive, among them Mary McMenamin, whose encouragement and dedication ensured that the final product was of high quality.

I also express my gratitude to the scholars who completed their dissertations and whose examples are included in this book as well as their faculty advisors who mentored them during the dissertation process.

Dissertation Title

The dissertation title briefly informs the reader of the content and intent of the researcher's study. According to the American Psychological Association (2010), "A title should be fully explanatory when standing alone. Although its principal function is to inform readers about the study, a title is also used as a statement of content for abstracting and information services, such as APA's *Pyschological Abstracts* and PsycINFO database" (p. 23). Use caution when selecting a title. A rambling title may not convey the essence of the study. The following questions guide the creation of an effective title:

Does the title identify the focus of the study's research?
Does the title convey the study's relevance and importance?
Does the title indicate the study's methodology?
Does the title contain only essential words?
Does the title use complete words [no abbreviations]?

Examples

- The power of appreciative inquiry: Discovering the latent potential of an urban high school (Miller, 2011)
- The influence of teacher characteristics on preference for models of teaching (McCord, 2010)
- The role of male partners in childbirth decision making: A qualitative exploration with first-time parenting couples (Dejoy, 2011)

Dissertation Abstract

The dissertation abstract is a brief description of the researcher's dissertation. It is accurate, self-contained, concise, and specific (American Psychological Association, 2010). The abstract requires the researcher to condense the study to less than two pages. Many dissertation abstracts are no more than 350 words; brevity is important. The abstract informs the reader about the study, methodology, results, and conclusions.

A well-written abstract condenses all of the essential parts of the study into a coherent whole. The following step-by-step guide identifies each part of the abstract construction process.

STEP 1: BEGIN THE ABSTRACT BY BRIEFLY RESTATING THE PROBLEM STATEMENT

Examples

Problem Statement

- This ethnographic-in-nature study explores how two middle school science teachers who have classes populated by urban African Americans teach their students and how their students perceive their teaching. (Bondima, 2004, para. 1)
- This study was conducted to investigate the possible relationship between exercise lifestyles and the overall experience of anxiety in a college setting. (Preiss, 2004, para. 1)
- This study examined emotion management skills in anxious children and their mothers and investigated factors within the child and the parent, and the child-parent relationship that may relate to the development of adaptive emotion management. (Suveg, 2003, para. 1)

STEP 2: PROVIDE A BRIEF RATIONALE OF WHY THE STUDY IS
IMPORTANT.

Example

- Current literature supports undergraduate research as a
  means of reaping positive benefits for both students and institutions. Since most of the studies concerning undergraduate
  research focus on quantitative data and outcomes, very little
  literature exists that explains how students experience the research process and what factors contribute to these positive
  outcomes. This dissertation focuses on the ways that performing research influences student engagement on campus. Ex-
  tending this concept of engagement, the study illuminates five
  areas that emerged in the literature—academic background,
  personal identity, sociocultural factors, institutional characteristics, and faculty interactions—that were conceived as having
  a reciprocal relationship with the student research process.
  (Krabacher, 2008, p. ii)
- The importance of college enrollment has surged as degrees
  have increasingly become prerequisites for employment.
  While enrollment numbers have risen, rates of attendance
  among all populations have not been equal. Low-income and
  first-generation students enroll and complete college at lower
  rates than their counterparts. Conducted during a psycholo-
  gy-based high school curriculum intervention designed to increase underrepresented students' likelihood of successful
  college completion, this qualitative inquiry used methods of
  grounded theory to provide insights into persisting inequal-
  ities in educational attainment. The study focused on poten-
  tially college-bound students' aspirations, perceptions, and
  views of their educational landscape with the aim to increase
  understanding of the academic attainment challenges some
  students from high poverty high schools. (Drotos, 2011)

STEP 3: IDENTIFY THE METHODOLOGY AND INCLUDE
VARIABLES, POPULATION, METHODS, AND DATA ANALYSIS

Example

- There were ten participants in the experimental (forgiveness education) group and ten participants in the control (alternative education) group. Participants had all been divorced or permanently separated for at least two years from their former abusive spouse or partner. Ages ranged from thirty-two to fifty-four years, with a mean age of 44.95 (SD = 7.01). A matched, yoked, randomized, experimental control group design was used. Participants were matched on age, duration of abusive relationship, time since permanent separation or divorce, current contact with the former abuser, and categories of psychological abuse. Each participant had weekly one-hour sessions (both forgiveness and alternative treatment) with the intervener based on a protocol specific to each treatment. The Enright Forgiveness Process Model was adapted to an intervention manual for this population as a protocol for the forgiveness intervention sessions. (Reed, 2004, para. 1)

STEP 4: IDENTIFY THE STUDY'S RESULTS/FINDINGS.

Example

- Regression analysis revealed that AS predicted depression over time, and each specific factor of AS predicted depression across time. A longitudinal relation between AS and panic approached significance across time, and the Mental Incapacitation Concerns and Social Concerns factors of AS significantly predicted panic endorsement over time. Panic severity and anxiolytic alcohol expectancies were not predicted by AS. Finally, AS scores were stable across time points, though small fluctuations in scores were noted. (Carpiniello, 2004, para. 2)

STEP 5: IDENTIFY THE STUDY'S CONCLUSIONS

Examples

- In summary, the results confirm that migraine sufferers are more sensitive to intense visual stimulation than controls, but do not support the contention that exposure results in widespread autonomic changes. Since interictal visual discomfort is common in migraine, further research is needed to clarify how it can be incorporated into models of migraine pathophysiology. (Crotogino, 2002, para. 5)
- Analysis of the data suggests a strong, positive relationship among (1) the nature of the change (a rebranding that was viewed positively by participants), (2) the credibility of the leaders was evident in their communication throughout the change process, and (3) the change communication process was perceived as well structured by participants. (Gradwell, 2004, para. 3)

Example: Complete Abstract

The purpose of this study was to examine the supervision and evaluation of principals by superintendents in light of accountability and low performing schools. The researcher sought to understand both the policy and implementation of principal evaluation through a survey administered to gain knowledge of implementation of policy. Superintendents from school systems across the state of Georgia (N = 146) were surveyed about their supervisory and evaluative practices related to principals of low performing, Title I schools before and after the school received the low performing ("in needs of improvement") status. Additionally, data were collected for superintendents' supervisory and evaluative practices of principals of Title I performing schools so that comparisons could be made. The mixed method approach allowed for the collection and analysis of qualitative and quantitative data. Structured interviews of five superintendents were conducted to gain perspectives of the superintendents' practices of supervision and evaluation of principals of Title I schools. The qualitative data collected from the interviews were combined with the current related literature of principal evaluation and supervision for the formulation of a survey instrument called the Survey of Superintendent's Supervisory and Evaluative Practices of Principals. The responses from the statewide survey plus demographic data were analyzed using both descriptive and inferential statistics. The findings of the qualitative data collected from the interviews (N = 5) aided in understanding the quantitative data collected from the surveys (N = 105) which yielded statistically significant results finding that both the superintendents' supervisory and evaluative practices changed after a Title I school became low performing. Moreover, superintendents' supervisory and evaluative practices of principals of Title I schools that remained performing did not change to the same degree as did for the low performing schools. The findings of the study will assist superintendents as they respond to schools in need of improvement and accountability policy mandates. For policy makers, an understanding of the supervisory and evaluative practices of superintendents in light of accountability are better understood. (Mattingly, 2003, p. 2)

ONE
Introduction and Rationale

Chapter 1 introduces the dissertation topic and presents the blue-print for the dissertation. The reader will use chapter 1 to understand the focus of the dissertation and the context in which it is framed and to preview the methodological approach the researcher took in conducting the research. The following components are often found in chapter 1:

- Introduction
- Background to the Study
- Problem Statement
- Purpose of the Study
- Significance of the Study
- Overview of Methodology
- Research Questions and/or Research Hypotheses
- Objectives and Outcomes
- Limitations
- Delimitations
- Assumptions
- Key Terms
- Organization of the Dissertation

Note: Always consult with your academic department and advisor for the required contents for your discipline.

INTRODUCTION

Chapter 1 is an introduction to the researcher's study. In the introduction, the researcher describes the broader context and issues surrounding the study. The researcher links the broader context, in a
general sense, to the question(s) the researcher wants to answer.
The researcher provides data and a rationale documenting the importance for the study (Walonick, 2005).

Examples

- The study of quantitative variation is of special interest to
  agricultural scientists since it tries to explain the variation and
  inheritance of many of the most important traits related to
  food and fiber production (e.g. yield, nutritional value, etc.).
  These traits are characterized by the multiple genes controlling them and their large environmental dependency. These
  factors complicate their study, but at the same time provide a
  challenge to understanding the complex genetic mechanisms
  that characterize these traits. (Uauy, 2007 p. 1)
- The aim of this study is to describe the direct or instrumental
  use of policy-relevant information in the policy making process of the Chilean secondary education reform carried out
  between 1995 and 2000. This is a very peculiar setting because
  of the strong background in social research of the policy makers who were in charge of the design and implementation of
  the reform policy. The result of this study provides a better
  understanding of the type of relationship between information and policymaking that occurs when researchers who are
  involved extensively with planning and carrying out underlying research also play the role of policymakers who both identify relevant problems and devise appropriate solutions. (Tellez, 2004, p. 1)

BACKGROUND TO THE STUDY

The background to the study narrows the focus of the introduction
and builds the case for the problem statement. The background
places the study in a historical context and connects it to its current
context. The researcher briefly describes the related research and

highlights key theoretical constructs the researcher will use to guide the study (Baron, 2005).

PROBLEM STATEMENT

The problem statement evolves out of the background and provides a well-constructed argument that adequate information is not available [a gap] to explain the problem or that a potential solution for the problem does not exist. It provides a rationale for examining prevailing ideas and knowledge with different theories or perspectives (World Health Organization, 2004). According to Clark, Guba, and Smith (1977), a problem "establishes the existence of two or more juxtaposed factors which, by their interaction, produce (1) an enigmatic or perplexing state, (2) yield an undesirable consequence, or (3) result in a conflict which renders the choice from among available alternatives moot" (p. 3). It concludes with a specific and well-constructed statement of the problem.

Examples

- Since the NDLTD surveys do not provide definitive answers on whether publishers will accept or reject articles submitted for publication and because no scientific research has been conducted in this area, in this study ETD university personnel are surveyed to determine if graduate student alumni are reporting publisher rejections for articles submitted for publication, because the articles were derived or taken directly from ETDs. (McCutcheon, 2010, p. 27)
- This researcher will examine the criteria that attract and matter most to parents and caregivers of African American children with respect to selection and preference when making a school choice in one particular integrated, magnet school district of choice. (Anderson, 2003, p. 2)

PURPOSE OF THE STUDY

> **Quick Tip:** The *purpose of the study* literally takes the summation of a concise *problem statement*, slightly rewording it to transform the *problem statement* into a *purpose of the study*. Always begin it this way: "The purpose of this [my] study is . . ."

The *purpose of the study* offers a precise summation of the study's overall purpose. It signifies the researcher's intent to address the problem. Once the researcher states the purpose, the researcher provides a rationale supporting the purpose of the study.

Examples

- The present study was designed for initial exploration regarding the relationship between various kinds of self-efficacy beliefs and purpose in life in a college student population. It was hypothesized that self-efficacy beliefs are significantly associated with purpose in life. Individuals reporting higher self-efficacy, especially beliefs relative to a college population (e.g., college, social, and general self-efficacy), would likely report greater purpose in life. (DeWitz, 2004, p. 10)
- The purpose of the current study was to conduct a comprehensive meta-analysis of the research on distance education in allied health science education. This meta-analysis investigated student achievement as well as student satisfaction resulting from distance education programs. Instructional design and delivery methods were investigated to determine components that contribute to the effectiveness of distance education. (Williams, 2004, p. 20)

SIGNIFICANCE OF THE STUDY

The *significance of the study* identifies how the study could make a significant and original contribution to the profession, the scholarly literature, and the researcher's discipline. It provides answers to why it is important to study the problem.

It is important to study the problem because it has the potential to influence policy and contribute to advancing research in the researcher's field of inquiry. According to the Agency for Healthcare Research and Quality (2005) the *significance of the study* provides:

> The current state of knowledge and potential contributions and significance of the research to the field. . . . [It] highlight(s) potential policy or practice impacts. Highlight(s) why research findings are important beyond the confines of the specific research project (e.g., significance; how research results can be applied).

Examples

- This study promises to add to the literature on general education by analyzing the status of general education at the end of the 20th century, and comparing these findings to the previous studies, (Toombs et al., 1989 and Gaff, 1991). Just as the Toombs and Gaff studies drew comparisons of their findings to previous studies, the present study extends the study of general education on a national level and contributes to a chronicle that describes how general education is evolving. Finally, the present study presents alternative models for examining general education and understanding how general education practice and research might be improved. This chapter established the need and purpose for the present study, summarized its research questions, its design, its assumptions and limitations, and provided definitions of key terms. The next chapter reviews selected literature representing the extant knowledge regarding general education curriculum and curriculum change over the period studied. (D. K. Johnson, 2002, p. 16)
- This study has significant implications for principals tasked with refreshing educational technology. The study provides in-depth information on site-level problems as well as solutions associated with the educational technology refresh process from a principal's perspective. (Denton, 2011, p. 5)

OVERVIEW OF METHODOLOGY

The researcher presents an overview of the methodology. The overview acts as an *executive summary* of the research design (Glatthorn, 1998). The overview describes:

- Methods used to collect data
- Research questions or hypotheses investigated
- Unit of analysis/subjects
- Method of assessment, observation, or evaluation
- Instruments involved in the assessment, observation, or evaluation of the subjects
- Procedures for data analysis

These sections are brief. The researcher provides a full explanation of these sections in later chapters.

Examples

- Based upon the overall research aim and specific research questions, the research involved a mixed methods study relating to factors influencing individual unlearning within work organizational contexts. A conceptual framework was built as a result of the analysis and synthesis of existing literature, and this framework was used to guide the research. (Becker, 2007, pp. 6–7)
- This research adapts probabilistic-based engineering tools and techniques to a food safety problem. While this research uses E. coli O157:H7 contamination in cheese for the application of this approach, it should be noted that the methodology developed in this research can be applied to any food-pathogen combination of interest. This chapter provides a general overview of the engineering risk assessment methodology developed in this research. In addition, a statement of the problem is given, as applied to E. coli O157:H7 in cheese; this statement includes the purpose, structure, scope/assumptions, and goals of the application. Finally, in order to better understand the application of the methodology, background information on cheese-making is provided. (Fretz, 2006, p. 24)

RESEARCH QUESTIONS

Research questions in qualitative studies seek to gather rich and descriptive information (Merriam, 2002). Research questions in a quantitative study seek numerical data. Yin (2003) maintains the secret to excellent research questions is their substance and form. Substance is the description of what the study is about, and form is the type of question the researcher asks. An appropriate research question might ask: What is the educational impact of the policy on student achievement?

Examples

- What are students' perceptions of their tutorial learning experiences? (Alexander, 2004, p. 34)
- RQ1: Is there a relationship between teacher perceptions of high school principals' monitoring student progress and stu-

dent achievement as measured by the *Performance Index* on Ohio's local report card data? (Chappelear, 2011, p. 5)

RESEARCH HYPOTHESES

Quantitative research requires a research hypothesis as an integral part of the study. Hypotheses identify the questions the researcher tests. The researcher uses the hypothesis to define and operationalize the study's variables. Moreover, the hypotheses create a link between the conceptual or theoretical framework and the research design (Clark et al., 1977).

The researcher typically uses a hypothesis to predict the outcome. The researcher sometimes refers to this hypothesis as the "alternative hypothesis." All other possible outcomes are referred to as the "null hypothesis" (Trochim, 2006).

Examples

- H8b: The perception that other field offices are using newer, more innovative data sets to inform biodiversity management decisions is positively associated with the selection of newer, more innovative data sets by a particular field office. (Gerlach, 2009, p. 61)
- H9a: High levels of public involvement in biodiversity management decisions at the field office level are positively associated with the selection of state and local government agency data. (Gerlach, 2009, p. 61)
- Hypothesis 1: Perceived importance of functional needs for snowboarders would have an impact on attitudes toward snowboarding helmets, controlling for other needs (i.e., expressive, aesthetic, and regulatory needs). (Chae, 2006, p. 7)

OBJECTIVES AND OUTCOMES

Objectives or outcomes are predictive and anticipated results from the study. The research objectives and/or outcomes present a summary of what the researcher intends to achieve through the study. The researcher generates research objectives and outcomes aligned with the study's theoretical and conceptual frameworks. Objectives or outcomes establish a relationship between the study's central question and the research questions or hypotheses and are linked to previous research (Clark et al., 1977).

Examples

- The specific objective of this dissertation is to study the control of the hydrodynamics and heat transfer in networks by means of theoretical, numerical, and experimental methods. (Franco, 2003, p. 20)
- Identify and describe competencies required for Extension professionals in Ohio to be successful now and in the future. (Cochran, 2009, p. 5)

LIMITATIONS

> **Quick Tip:** Be accurate, honest, and forthright in acknowledging limita tions. It is a mark of researcher integrity.

"Design flaws are called limitations and they are what you should write about under the first subheading of this section. The researcher briefly identifies and presents known flaws in the research design" (Murillo, 2005). Limitations identify potential weaknesses in the study's research design or methodology restricting the study's scope (Colorado State University School of Education, 2001). The researcher anticipates limitations in the study's design and offers a plan to minimize the effect of the limitations (Karchmer, 1996).

Examples

- Because the teaching process is both complex and dynamic (Cochran-Smith and Lytle, 1990), it is implicit that the responses provided by participants will be contextually influenced and multifaceted in nature. In addition, it is assumed that participants' knowledge of gifted students' specialized learning needs and understanding of the models of teaching have been influenced and enhanced by the professional development training that participants received during grant dissemination. (McCord, 2010, pp. 16–17)
- The limitations of the present study involve participant sampling and lack of theoretical saturation; limited involvement

of participants in theory development and revision; uneven degree of meaning unit analysis; idiosyncratic aspects of investigator bias; and the unique nature of bias toward social acceptability in therapists. (Baehr, 2004, pp. 327–28)

DELIMITATIONS

Delimitations are the boundaries to narrow the scope of the study (Baron, 2005). The researcher delimits the study when the researcher chooses to include or exclude as a means of defining the study's boundaries.

Examples

- The classrooms for this study were selected from a typical alternative education school in Miami, Florida. Delimitations exist by specifying teachers and students in alternative education classrooms as the population of this study. The results of this study do not necessarily generalize to other populations from other alternative schools in other school districts. Alternative education schools in Miami, Florida, are situated and defined in this study according to the definition of urban contexts in the K–12 education literature. Urban contexts in the K–12 education literature are represented as populated with students of color in lower income settings with meager resources and imposing bureaucracies. In light of these definitions, this study focused on what happens in classrooms with students who have been suspended or expelled from their regular urban school for disruptive or juvenile delinquent behavior, disproportionately African American and Latino, or non-dominant, students. (Pane, 2009, pp. 13–14)
- Constraints imposed by the researcher are as follows: Data representing participants are limited to graduates enrolled in the pre-licensure full-time and part-time programs who enrolled to start nursing coursework during the fall 2005 through graduation in spring 2009. A limited number of variables that impacted participants' success were examined in this study. Variables not examined included: ACT scores, remedial course work, Mosby Assess Test, and the NET test (were not utilized at the time of study). (Strayer, 2010, p. 15).

ASSUMPTIONS

Assumptions are formed by the researcher's underlying beliefs and values. According to Kennedy (2004), "In research, assumptions are equivalent to axioms in geometry—self-evident truths, the sine qua non of research" (characteristic 6, para. 1). An axiom is, "What you ask determines what you'll find." The initial question determines the focus of the inquiry and is driven by the researcher's assumptions regarding the study. In research, well-constructed assumptions add to the study's legitimacy. Some researchers, such as Yin (2003), refer to assumptions as "propositions."

Examples

- Assumed is the idea that, if resistance to inclusive programs is to be avoided, attention needs to be directed toward identifying perceived needs of special and general classroom teachers working in inclusive settings. As such, special and general classroom educators are important informants about the availability of resources and support needed for implementing inclusive education. (Luseno, 2001, p. 3)
- The trustworthiness of the study is based on a set of assumptions and for the sake of disclosure is set forth. It is extremely important that respondents answer accurately to describe their practice in context. Evidence exists that the superintendents are concerned with improving technology use in their Montana K–12 schools and using electronic technology to be more efficient. This research design presumes superintendents make decisions regarding technology, have a planning process, and use technology for diversified purposes. Furthermore, there is an assumption that superintendents have individual beliefs regarding technology efficacy in K–12 public schools and that these beliefs guide their approaches in practice. Although it cannot be predicted what issues, perceptions, or theories will emerge, an assumption that there is an important relationship between assumptions and technology use exists. Additionally, it is assumed that technology has affected superintendents' political, instructional, and managerial roles. (Anderson, 2009, p. 16)

DEFINITION OF KEY TERMS

Key terms refer to the specific terms central to the study and used throughout the dissertation. Key terms are accurate, devoid of ambiguity, and seek to explain terms that may be vague or have a contextually related meaning (Georgia Institute of Technology School of Civil and Environmental Engineering, 2001). Typically, researchers include key terms that identify and explain the independent, dependent, and control variables (University of San Francisco, 2004). List the terms in alphabetical order, with citations where appropriate.

Examples

- Collective efficacy refers to a group's beliefs and perceptions "concerned with the performance capability of a social system as a whole" (Bandura, 1997, p. 469). (Gage, 2003, p. 183)
- Middle School—A school unit that follows the elementary unit and precedes the high school unit; includes students from grades six, seven, and eight of a graded school organization (Eichhorn, 1966, p. 107). (C. Miller, 2004, p. 5)

ORGANIZATION OF THE DISSERTATION

This concluding section of chapter 1 presents a brief executive summary of the remainder of the dissertation. The organization of the dissertation begins by describing the dissertation's format and the content found in subsequent chapters of the dissertation.

Examples

- Chapter 1 introduced the statement of the problem, purpose of the study, the importance of the study, limitations, and delimitations. Additionally, the conceptual basis of the study was established. The research questions were also clarified. Chapter 2 contains literature and research related to the broad topics that contain altruism and emotional intelligence. These topics are leadership and motivation. Methodology for this study is presented in chapter 3 and includes the research design, selection of the sample, data collection tasks, and data analysis procedures. Results obtained from this method are available in chapter 4. The final chapter, chapter 5, is a discussion of the study. (L. Miller, 2003)

- This applied research study is divided into five chapters. The first chapter provides an introduction to the study, the statement of the problem, research questions, the conceptual framework used in the study, and the significance of the study for future public policy. The second chapter reviews the literature as it pertains to the need and value of dual enrollment programs, a summary of existing dual enrollment models and policies, and Astin's I-E-O Model. The third chapter discusses the research design, variables, and statistical procedures used to answer each of the posed research questions. Chapter four details the results of the study for each of the research questions and chapter five discusses the results, their implications for higher education and state policy, and recommendations for future research on Ohio's Postsecondary Enrollment Options Program. (Geise, 2011, p. 9)

Pep Talk

Make a commitment: thirty minutes of uninterrupted time *every day* until chapter 1 is completed. WRITE! WRITE! WRITE! WRITE!

You must do the thing you think you cannot do.
—Eleanor Roosevelt

TWO

Review of Literature

Chapter 2 presents a review of the relevant literature related to the researcher's essential question(s) or hypotheses of the dissertation. It contains the theory and empirical research that serve as the foundation for the study. It also provides evidence that the line of inquiry is grounded in a solid theoretical and empirical research foundation by identifying areas of agreement, argument, and lack of knowledge in the researcher's dissertation's question(s) or hypotheses. The following components are often found in chapter 2:

- Introduction to the Literature Review
- Body of the Literature Review
- Competing Perspectives
- Conceptual Framework
- Theoretical Framework
- Synthesis of the Research
- Critical Analysis
- Conclusion of the Literature Review

Note: Always consult with your academic department and advisor for the required contents for your discipline.

After I present the *Essential Elements* of chapter 2, I present two special sections:

1. Essential Definitions Guiding the Literature Review
2. Strategies for Conducting the Literature Review

I strongly recommend using strategies associated with the systemic literature review presented in this section.

ORGANIZING THE LITERATURE REVIEW

Quick Tip: The software I use in preparing to write is iMindmap. Mindmapping is an effective and efficient way to creatively organize thinking before beginning to write.

This chapter provides a clear understanding of how to go about conducting a literature review and a suggested organizational schema for the dissertation. It can be broken into three basic components: *introduction, body, and conclusion* (University of Wisconsin–Madison Writing Center, 2004). The researcher categorizes and comments on what recognized scholars and researchers contributed through their published empirical or theoretical work. The literature review is organized according to a logical and defensible schema (Taylor, 2001).

A literature review reports published primary scholarship. The scholarship may be empirical, theoretical, critical/analytic, or methodological. According to Afolabi (1992), the literature review includes landmark studies and contains a critical analysis of pertinent work. The researcher

- Identifies critical variables and identifies important relationships among them
- Synthesizes findings
- Confirms the problem context and its significance
- Places the study's research into a proper perspective

INTRODUCTION TO THE LITERATURE REVIEW

In the introduction to the literature review, the researcher establishes boundaries for the literature review. Boundaries restrict the literature review to studies germane to the researcher's research topic, provide an overall organization of the review, and identify the criteria used to evaluate the scholarly literature (University of Wisconsin–Madison Writing Center, 2004). Often researchers subdivide the literature review into major sections with section summaries and a chapter summary.

Examples

- This chapter will begin with a review of the literature, which addresses variables that predict outcome in marital therapy. Next, the empirical studies on shame and perception of health in the family of origin will be reviewed. Finally, the sociodemographic variables that predict divorce will be addressed. The purpose of this review is to provide an understanding of the previous research in this area, as well as providing a rationale for the choice of predictor variables in the present study. (Horak, 2002, p. 16)
- The guiding developmental theory for this work is that of Daniel Levinson. His work in this area was influenced by the work of Erik Erikson and his conception of ego stages across the life cycle (Levinson, 1986). Specifically, it was the view of "the engagement of self with world" (Levinson, 1986, p. 3) across the life cycle that most caught Levinson's attention. Erikson's model of the adult life cycle consists of three stages beyond childhood: intimacy versus isolation, generativity versus stagnation, and integrity versus despair (Erikson, 1982). Each of these stages emphasizes a relationship of self with the world. When compared to Levinson's model, Erikson's intimacy versus isolation roughly compares to Levinson's era of early adulthood; generativity versus stagnation compares to era of middle adulthood; and integrity versus despair compares to era of late adulthood. Erikson does not assign age delineation; Levinson does. This is one primary difference between the two theories. (Allgood, 2003, p. 17)
- This chapter presents a review of research and literature on students with Specific Learning Disabilities (SLD) and Alcohol, Tobacco, and Other Drug (ATOD) use, the development of social and resiliency skills by students with SLD, and demographics of students with SLD. Items selected for review address each of the characteristics identified for this exploratory study. The first review area includes a discussion of the definitions of special learning disabilities; facts and figures about learning disabilities in the United States; interpersonal, communication, and learning skills related to SLD; perceptions and problem-solving skills related to learning disabilities; al-

cohol-related issues with learning disabilities; mental health issues; and gender findings relating to learning disabilities. The second area includes discussion of skill development and prevention programming relating to learning disabilities. (Smith, 2004, p. 19)

BODY OF THE LITERATURE REVIEW

The body of the literature review assimilates and synthesizes the scholarly literature germane to the study's topic. Researchers often organize the body of the literature review into subsections (D'Angelo, 2002). The organization may take one or a combination of the following formats:

- Theory
- Methodology
- Chronology
- Ideology
- Themes
- Findings
- Populations studied

The body of the literature review may also include

- Competing perspectives
- Conceptual framework
- Theoretical framework
- Synthesis of the research
- Critical analysis

COMPETING THEORETICAL PERSPECTIVES

An important component of the body of the literature review is an acknowledgment of the different theoretical perspectives related to the study. Most theoretical perspectives can be divided into four subsections (Yin, 2003):

1. Individual
2. Group
3. Societal
4. Organizational

Examples

- Some researchers argue that race plays the primary role in creating and maintaining current patterns of segregation between black and white households (Denton and Massey, 1988; Immergluck, 1998; Kain, 1987), while others contend that the racial gap in homeownership has more to do with groups' economic disparities than with the persistence of racial discrimination (Wilson, 1987). According to Wilson's arguments, the decreased ability of black compared to white families to purchase a home is reflected in segregated neighborhoods, because some residential areas require more money to move into them than others (i.e., more expensive homes). For those who believe forms of racial discrimination continue to shape where blacks and whites live in relation to each other, these average economic differences do little to explain persistent segregation levels in the US. Regardless of which factor one considers to be the primary reason behind residential segregation, all agree that current housing patterns exist within the larger context of history, societal prejudices, and government policies. "Housing conditions are basically the result of the interrelation between resources of households, preferences of households, and the availability and accessibility of dwellings" (van Kempen and Ozuekren, 1998). (Bond, 2004, p. 6)
- Next I review and contrast two competing theoretical perspectives on aging: life stage and life course theories. I then elaborate on the theoretical frame I use to examine musicians' life course developments, particularly during their transition to adulthood. I conclude by discussing the contributions my research will make to various subareas of sociology more generally. (Ramirez, 2007, p. 21)

CONCEPTUAL FRAMEWORK

A *conceptual framework* has its genesis in the ideas, constructs, experiences, and facts surrounding the study (Krumme, 2002). Miles and Huberman (1994) define a conceptual framework as an explanation of the relationship among the study's *factors, constructs,* or *key variables.* The researcher's use of a conceptual framework provides support for the identification of a theoretical model to guide the researcher's study (Salem, 2004).

Examples

- The conceptual framework developed here is based on an exploration of the relationship between people and the environment. We postulate that (1) the environment can be described in terms of its components (biophysical, structural, activities and general community elements); (2) human beings have a relationship with the environment that can be affective-sensory (attachment by identity, peacefulness, security, sociability, beauty) or functional-instrumental (removal or harvesting, pollution, development, access or distribution, nuisance, cultural relations, recreational functions); (3) human beings assess their environmental quality of life based on the satisfaction of these basic needs and personal requirements, attitude, experience of, and attachment to the space, cultural and historical relationships with the environment, the investment made to achieve the current level of quality of life, and the comparison they draw between their situation and that of other groups; and, finally, (4) relationships with the environment are associated with individual characteristics like age, gender, health, education, income, ethnic origin, and marginality. (Andre, Bitondo, Berthelot, and Louillet, 2001, sec. 5, para. 1)

- The first goal of the research therefore became to create a model synthesizing existing frameworks and enable as encompassing and consistent a description of mediated environments to be conducted as possible. In the creation of the framework, more than thirty separate classification systems, lists, and frameworks were drawn upon and blended. Additional categories were added based on the responses of participants engaged in the pilot study and through the various case studies. Feedback from journal reviewers and conference delegates as well as discussions with friends and colleagues informed its development. Hence, the framework was formed: (1) Including all of the various concepts encountered during the literature review regarding mediated environments in order to create a framework that incorporates all other frameworks encountered. (2) Merging or dividing these concepts, where appropriate, to create clear distinct categories, eliminate redundancy as much as possible. This and the previous criterion conform to the principle in forming categories of "parsimony of variables and formulation and scope in the applicability" (Merriam, 1998; 191). (3) Developing a self-consistent nomenclature, adopting existing terms where these are commonly employed or inventing new ones where existing ones were too ambiguous. (Childs, 2010, p. 24)

THEORETICAL FRAMEWORK

> **Quick Tip:** The theoretical framework chosen frames the researcher's line of inquiry. View it as complementary and adding to other theoretical perspectives.

The theoretical framework is comprised of long-standing theoretical traditions, theoretical principles and their relationship (Krumme, 2000). The researcher chooses a theoretical framework based on personal preference. Once the researcher makes a decision on a theory, the researcher constructs the theoretical framework.

The theoretical framework connects to the problem statement and addresses the research questions or hypotheses explaining and defending the approach to the researcher's line of inquiry. The researcher asks:

1. How does the theory provide an explanation for what is happening?
2. What other theory(s) provide an alternative explanation?

Examples

- I have identified three different strands of literature that relate to calling. The first is the literature that directly addresses calling or the experiences that accompany it. This strand includes several writers from different time periods whom I have arranged in a chronological sequence to get a feel for historical shifts in thinking about the phenomenon of calling. Second, I have chosen to review literature on motivational theory that I believe relates to the phenomenon of calling. Last, I have taken a look at writers who address adult education organizational issues that I believe relate to the way one perceives calling. (Collins, 2004, p. 16)
- Black feminism was chosen as the theoretical perspective for this study because it identifies the nuances of race and gender in the lives and experiences of African American women. Black feminism, defined by Collins (1990) as "the process of

self-conscious struggle that empowers women and men to re-
alize a humanistic vision of community," suggests that
"African American women as a group experience a world different from that of those who are not Black and female and
that these experiences stimulate a distinctive Black feminist
consciousness" (Collins, 1990, p. 24). (Beloney-Morrison, 2003,
p. 29)

- Theoretical Framework: Radical Change Theory. The theory
of Radical Change was developed in the field of Library and
Information Studies (LIS) by Eliza T. Dresang. The theory explains that contemporary youth information resources and behaviors experience transformations in ways that reflect the
properties of the digital age. In the 1990s when the theory was
developed, the digital age clearly emerged and digital media
such as personal computers with Internet connectivity had
started to permeate the lives of the general populace. Society
became increasingly more interactive and connected through
digital networks. Radical Change indicated fundamental
changes in the new era, departing from the usual or traditional in information resources or behaviors, although still related
to it (Dresang, 1999). (Koh, 2011, p. 4)

SYNTHESIS OF THE RESEARCH

A synthesis of the research indicates how existing research supports
or does not support existing theories and questions (Colorado State
University School of Education, 2001). In this subsection, the researcher makes sense of the research by identifying *patterns, themes,
common findings*, and *gaps*.

CRITICAL ANALYSIS

The researcher applies a critical analysis to evaluate the research. In
the discussion of the research, the researcher presents the strengths
and weaknesses of the relevant empirical research providing evidence for the quality of the research designs and the overall quality
of the research (LeJeune, 2001). In effect, the researcher constructs
an argument for the researcher's study to advance what is already
known (Ormondroyd, Engle, and Cosgrave, 2004).

CONCLUSION OF THE LITERATURE REVIEW

The researcher concludes the literature review with a summary of the salient sections of the literature in the order they were addressed in the chapter. Depending on the norms in the researcher's academic department, the researcher may also introduce the forthcoming chapter on methodology.

Examples

- This chapter reviewed the literature about how and why women are not equitably represented in educational administrative positions within our nation's secondary schools. In addition, this chapter attempted to illustrate that women tend to lead learning institutions in particular ways. Traditional bureaucratic organizational structures have focused on masculine characteristics. The call for more transformational styles of leadership, which has dominated recent literature regarding successful school leadership, has promoted the "reinvention" of today's principal. Furthermore, research conducted in the last few decades has shed light on successful leadership approaches that draw from the research on women's styles of leading. Finally, the way principals are evaluated has recently been reformed based on ISLLC Standards in ways that resonate with feministic aspects of leadership. (Thurman, 2004, p. 34)
- Regardless of what causes them, it is well documented that poverty and inequity in the United States exist, and that they affect people's quality of life. Also, the way in which both poverty and inequity are examined and measured affects the evaluation of quality of life (UNDP, 1990). This study uses the human development index (HDI) of the United Nations Development Program (UNDP) to measure the quality of life of single mothers on welfare in Georgia, and of the Georgia population as a whole by race and county. The next chapter explains in detail the HDI. (Alzate, 2002, pp. 47–48)

ESSENTIAL DEFINITIONS GUIDING THE LITERATURE REVIEW

The following sections provide insight into critical components that assist the researcher in writing chapter 2: *theory, scholarly publications, relevant research, criteria for selection of research,* and *organizing the literature review.*

Theory

"Theory incorporates a set of well-developed concepts related through statements of relationship, which together constitute an integrated framework that can be used to explain or predict phenomena" (Strauss and Corbin, 1990, p. 15). One of the researcher's challenges is to present theory in a clear and succinct manner (Feldman, 2003). The researcher needs to be *clear, precise,* and *succinct* when defining the theoretical constructs relevant to the dissertation.

Scholarly Publications

The researcher distinguishes *scholarly* from *nonscholarly* works. A scholarly publication publishes original research by a researcher in the discipline, using appropriate references and citations, and addressing a research question or topic relevant to the publication's discipline (Engle, 2003). Since there is disparity in scholarly publications, refereed journals are more credible than nonrefereed journals. There is also a hierarchy among refereed journals. When in doubt about the quality of the journal, the researcher should consult with the dissertation advisor.

Relevant Research

> **Quick Tip:** Research is interesting and grabs your attention. Be alert, it may take your focus off your goal. If the research isn't relevant to your study, discard it and place it in a digital file for reading *after* the dissertation is successfully defended.

Relevant research has direct implications for the problem statement and research questions. The researcher follows the progression and evolution of research in the researcher's line of inquiry.

Examples

- The following literature review examines the relationship of professional development to teacher effectiveness in urban middle schools through the theoretical frameworks of organizational culture, organizational change (Schein, 2004), adult learning (Knowles, 1984), and professional development (Zepeda, 1999). We organized this literature review as follows: we framed the issue of teacher professional development in the theoretical constructs of organizational culture as it influences teacher competence in the classroom. As we examined the notion of organizational culture we looked at the theoretical constructs of organizational culture since it may impact the notion of teacher competence (Sarason, 1996). We then examined the process of change within the organizational culture. In this study, organizational culture and organizational change are reflective of organizations in general and educational organizations in particular. Within this framework, we examined the notion of adult learning, and then narrowed the focus to professional development for teachers in middle schools (Calabrese, Sheppard, Hummel, Laramore, and Nance, 2005, p. 10).

Another researcher introduced the section on relevant research this way: "The next section reviews the relevant research of compulsivity and compulsive buying with a discussion of definitions and the associated demographic, psychographic, and personality variables" (Workman, 2010, p. 24).

Strategies for Conducting the Literature review

Criteria for Selection of Research Included in a Literature Review

A challenge for researchers working on the literature review is the dilemma of how to select research to include in the literature review. The challenge is confounded by the exponential increase in the availability of scholarly published works as well as other related Internet materials. In the following paragraphs, I address the following questions:

- What literature do I review?
- How do I review it?
- What do I exclude?

Begin simplifying the process by establishing criteria for selection for inclusion at the onset of the literature review.

There are two approaches for establishing criteria for selection for inclusion in the literature review.

Approach 1: Critical Analysis of Information Sources.

A critical analysis of information sources has two phases: (1) a preliminary appraisal and (2) a content analysis (Ormondroyd, 2003).

Phase 1, the preliminary appraisal, is a crucial filter. Researchers include all relevant and scholarly information that meets the academic norms for their discipline. Using this strategy, the researcher collects as much information from as many different sources as possible related to the study. The information is assessed against the criteria for selection for inclusion. Once the initial appraisal is made, filter the remaining research by examining the authors' credentials, the quality of the scholarly sources, and the depth of the authors' research (Neuendorf, 2001). Scholarly research that passes through this filter moves to Phase 2.

Phase 2 is the content analysis, which examines the purpose and substance of each scholarly work. The content analysis examines the author's credentials for doing the study, the author's propositions for the study, the research questions, the depth of the literature review, the methodology, the legitimacy of the data analysis, and the results and conclusions the author makes based on the data analysis (Ormondroyd et al., 2004).

Based on the content analysis, the researcher sorts the surviving scholarly works into predetermined categories. The researcher may choose to base the categories on methodology, chronology, theme, researcher, organization, theory, or other relevant premises. Once the researcher separates the information into categories, the researcher assimilates, summarizes, and synthesizes the information and draws appropriate conclusions.

Approach 2: Adapting the Systematic Review of the Literature

Adapting the methods used in a systematic literature review is a way to establish criteria for selection for inclusion. A systematic literature review answers research questions and has a defensible methodology for searching the literature, selecting studies, and evaluating the selected studies. The following is an excellent statement on *the purpose of a systematic literature review* :

> The purpose of a systematic literature review is to evaluate and interpret all available research evidence relevant to a particular question. In this approach a concerted attempt is made to identify all relevant primary research, a standardized appraisal of study quality is made, and the studies of acceptable quality are systematically (and sometimes quantitatively) synthesized. This differs from a traditional review in which previous work is described but not systematically identified, assessed for quality, and synthesized. (National Health and Medical Research Council, 2000, p. 2)

The researcher restates the purpose of the study and identifies the juxtaposed positions poised in the problem statement. In the following hypothetical example, the researcher names the three variables in the study. By naming the variables, the researcher identifies the primary search terms for the literature review. Once the researcher identifies the search terms, the researcher distinguishes relevant databases to use in the search (see below) and the criteria to use in searching the databases. The researcher then sets the standard for inclusion in the literature review.

Examples: Systematic Literature

The proposed literature search aims to *identify, assimilate, summarize,* and *synthesize* all studies that report on the association between _____, _____, and _____. The following databases were used: _____, _____, and _____. Only full articles reviewed by the researcher are included in the literature review. An extended database search will be conducted based on author, title, and keywords using criteria as listed. The criteria used for this literature review include: (1) empirical studies conducted since _____; (2) empirical studies involving the following populations: _____, _____, and _____; and (3) empirical studies published in highly respected peer reviewed journals.

Examples: Systematic Literature

Review Protocols The systematic literature review (SLR) applied protocols that involved a series of decisions as to which literature would be searched and which pieces of literature would be selected for review. The first protocol was the literature source. It was felt that "pop" reports and opinion pieces were not appropriate to include in an SLR. An extensive search of the literature after consultation with the university research librarian suggested using electronic search mechanisms such as ERIC SilverPlatter, Wilson Select, ArticleFirst, ABI/INFORM, and Expanded Academic ASAP. Only literature driven by a research methodology would be included. Only literature having a salient bearing on the research question would be included (Calabrese, Sherwood, Fast, and Womack, 2003, p. 10).

Organizing the Literature Research Search

The researcher organizes the data accumulated from the search of scholarly publications to eliminate the chaos evident in stacks of papers, books, pamphlets, and bookmarked Internet sites.

Process for Selection for Inclusion in a Systematic Literature Review

1. Define the selection process (weighting and evaluating).
2. Identify the research question(s) being addressed in the systematic literature review.
3. Identify the criteria for selection of research studies and the studies' relationship to the research question(s).
4. Identify the criteria for exclusion of research studies. (Kitchenham, 2004)

The following is an example of how Dustin Miller identified a timeline for empirical research in his literature review. Crafting such a timeline organizes the writing of the literature review, provides a visual for the reader, and allows the researcher to understand the flow of empirical research as it relates to the researcher's study.

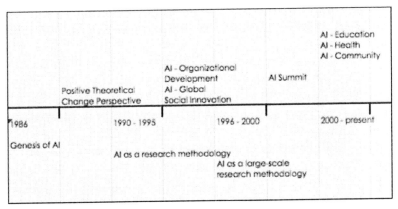

Figure 2.1. The timeline of appreciative inquiry (AI) gives an overview of AI since its inception in 1986. Since it first appeared in a doctoral dissertation, AI has been used as positive theoretical change perspective (the late 1980s to the present), a research methodology (early 1990s to the present), and a large-scale research methodology (mid-1990s to the present) in the form of an AI Summit. Over the last twenty-five years, AI has been found in business, education, health, community, and other social organizations. (D. Miller, 2011, p. 36)

Pep Talk

Commitment to take on a deep and substantive literature review will transform the researcher's knowledge base. The researcher becomes an authority on the study and advances current knowledge. Focus—allow no distractions!

The man [woman] who does things makes many mistakes, but he [she] never makes the biggest mistake of all—doing nothing.
—Benjamin Franklin

THREE

Methods

Chapter 3 presents the methods that the researcher uses to collect and analyze data for the study. The researcher describes the research perspective, research design and its limitations, subjects, research variables, instruments and measures of data collection, data analysis, and validity, and reliability and/or triangulation, as well as the methods used in the study (Karchmer and Johnson, 1996). The researcher describes the methodology in sufficient detail so others may replicate the study (Bradley, Flathouse, Gould, Hendricks, and Robinson, 1994).

The following components are often found in chapter 3:

- Introduction
- Research Perspective
- Research Design
- Research Questions and/or Hypotheses
- Subjects, Participants, Population, and Sample [Sometimes referred to as the Unit of Analysis]
- Research Variables
- Research Instrument
- Pilot Study
- Data Collection Procedures
- Data Collection and Statistical Analysis
- Setting and Environment
- Bias and Error
- Validity
- Trustworthiness

- Reliability
- Summary

Note: Always consult with your academic department and advisor for the required contents for your discipline.

INTRODUCTION

The introduction provides an overview and organization for chapter 3. In some dissertations, researchers replicate the rationale for the study, explanation of the context, and research questions or hypotheses from chapter 1 — this approach serves to tie the chapters together and maintain a consistency.

Examples

- This chapter describes the research methodology, methods, and materials for this study. It provides a comparison of the two research sites selected and a rationale for their selection. The use of symbolic interaction to study leadership is included, as well as a description of the methods used to collect and analyze data. The application of backward mapping to this study is explained. (Gohn, 2004, p. 28)
- The purpose of this study was to compare and evaluate the preferences of individuals who viewed two different approaches to counseling. In one approach, a multisensory Rational Emotive Behavior Therapy (REBT) approach was used and in the other a traditional Rational Emotive Behavior Therapy approach was used. This experimentally designed study consisted of participants observing two videotaped counseling interviews. This chapter consists of descriptions of the participants, stimulus materials, procedures, instrumentation, hypotheses, and the research design used in this study. (Cain, 2003, p. 30)
- This chapter highlights the research methodology and procedures used in the study, which consists of the following sections: purpose and objectives of the study, population and sample, instrument development and testing, methods and procedures, and data analysis. (Shao, 2004, p. 43)

RESEARCH PERSPECTIVE

Quick Tip: The research perspective frames the type of data collected and the research design.

The research perspective may be a phenomenological, scientific, positivist, naturalistic, reductionism, or a descriptive perspective. The research perspective limits the scope of the study and informs the reader of the boundaries within which the study will be conducted (Yin, 2003).

Examples

- This research study was guided by the phenomenological inquiry approach. Since this study aimed at understanding the perceptions and experiences of teachers from their own point of view, phenomenology was an ideal guiding framework as it is committed to understanding phenomenon from the actors perspective. . . . In addition, phenomenological inquiry focuses on the question, "What is the structure and essence of experience of this phenomenon for these people?" (Patton, 1990) and the study sought to understand the structure and experiences of the participants. (Wabuyele, 2003, p. 70)

- An appropriate research perspective is needed which can adequately represent these complex and dynamic entities and which can then address their conditions of success. A social network structural perspective is chosen in reference to that purpose. Studies of social network structure have been conducted since the 1930s in the social sciences, and, more recently, are gaining prominence in many fields, ranging from corporate strategy to network-based physics. A social network perspective focuses on the nature and structure of the relationships between social entities, rather than the attributes of the entities themselves. The social structuralist perspective is useful because it provides a unifying framework for a wide range of interdisciplinary concepts, and it also allows for the precise definition of constructs and the quantitative investigation of success factors. (Hinds, 2008, pp. 5–6)

- An alternative to the problem-based, deficit approach is an appreciative inquiry research perspective that focuses on the aspirations of stakeholders where the stakeholders' aspirations are their dreams and ambitions. The positive nature of an appreciative inquiry approach was represented in this study through its influence on the methodology. The central premise of appreciative inquiry is a focus on the generative capacity of the organization under study to define and envision the stakeholders' aspirations based on the community's inherent assets (Cooperrider and Srivastva, 1987). Generative capacity is defined as the ability of the subjects, not outside experts, to identify and mobilize resources from within the community of study (Hall and Hammond, 1998). Cooperrider and Watkins (2000) cited the results on medical patients who focused on generating positive mental images and thoughts. These patients made a faster recovery. Cooperrider and Watkins assert that focusing on the generative capacity of the subjects under study allows the subjects to feel empowered and to shape their future. (Fast, 2005, pp. 14–15)

RESEARCH DESIGN

> **Quick Tip:** Begin this section with a strong declarative sentence, for example, "I am using a qualitative embedded case study research design."

The research design provides the reader with the study's structure, detailing the methods to collect, record, and analyze data (Joppe, 2004). It is the blueprint for the research to answer the hypotheses/research questions. It may include:

- The problem statement
- The purpose of the study
- The research perspectives/theory
- The hypotheses/research questions
- The variables
- Operational definitions
- Methodology
- Data gathering and analysis
- Results/findings

Example

- The design selected for this investigation was a cross sectional design. Because the study proposed to investigate the effects of preservice teacher education on teachers' beliefs and attitudes about teaching culturally and linguistically diverse learners, comparing groups was necessary to document the changes, if any, in beliefs and attitudes. Cross sectional designs involve collecting data at one point in time from groups different in age and/or experience (Krathwohl, 1997; Wiersma, 2000). These designs are not suitable for measuring change in an individual. However, differences between selected groups in a cross-sectional study may represent changes that take place in a larger defined population (Wiersma, 2000). Notation of the study is

$$N \quad EG1 \quad O1 \quad O2 \quad O3 \quad X$$
$$N \quad EG2 \quad X \quad O1 \quad O2 \quad O3$$

RESEARCH QUESTIONS AND HYPOTHESES

In this section, the researcher restates the research questions or hypotheses that were presented in chapter 1. Research questions often are formed as how, what, or why questions. They are similar to hypotheses; however, a hypothesis is exact and indicates the measurement and analysis needed to address the hypothesis (Merriam, 2001; Yin, 2003).

Examples: Hypotheses

- H01: There will be no statistically significant relationships between midlevel managers' perceived utility of community-based programming and NCCCS institutional location, size, and unit. (Adams, 2002, p. 34)
- Hypothesis 2—Friendship Termination. Friendships between two delinquent adolescents and friendships between two nondelinquent adolescents will terminate less often than friendships between adolescents who do not share the same delinquency status. (Ackerman, 2003, p. 72)
- Based on arguments presented throughout these three chapters, net deficits in both trade deficits and FDI in a given country should, all else being equal, reduce demand for labor. Therefore, I expect the relationships between my measures of net deficits in trade and investment on the one hand, and

unemployment rates on the other, to be positive. (Ammon, 2002, p. 43)

Examples: Research Questions

- How do preservice teachers learn from early field experiences? (Olson, 2004, p. 5)
- How do preservice teachers begin the process of learning to teach as they move from university to schools? (Olson, 2004, p. 5)
- How does the community college culture from the students' perspective contribute to retention during the first six weeks of attendance? (Rasmussen, 2004, p. 6)
- How does the community college culture from the students' perspective contribute to non-retention during the first six weeks of attendance? (Rasmussen, 2004, p. 6)

SUBJECTS, PARTICIPANTS, POPULATION, AND SAMPLE

In this section, the researcher describes the study's subjects, the process used to select subjects, and reasons for withdrawal from the study. The researcher provides a clear description of the subjects. If the subjects dropped out of the study, the researcher provides the number of dropouts and the reasons for their withdrawal.

Examples

- Although I collected data within my research journal, participant observations, document analysis, and field notes from a much larger cross section of the school population, my key research participants in this tribal critical race theory (TribCrit) ethnographic study included twenty-two middle school educators. These educators included members of all six teaching teams, taught a wide array of academic and elective courses, worked as administrative faculty or school counseling staff, and served as support staff from multiple departments. Teaching teams at every grade level included a group of six to eight educators who taught a combination of mathematics, language arts, science, modern languages, social studies, communication arts, arts and technology, physical education, special education, music, and counseling. The participants were chosen from each of the content areas to gain as diverse a representation of educators as possible. (Abercrombie-Donahue, 2011, p. 62)

- The population studied consisted of the students at Stonewall Jackson Middle School (SJMS) in Charleston, West Virginia. The school enrollment at the time of the study was approximately six hundred students, 70 percent of whom were on free or reduced lunch, 30 percent were in special education, and 30 percent were minority, primarily black. From this group, a list of students was identified from the Kanawha County Schools student database that included all SJMS sixth and seventh grade students from the school year 2003–2004. Another list of students was identified as all SJMS students in the seventh and eighth grade for the school year 2004–2005. The Combined Group sample included all students who are on both lists, a total of 279 students. Group One (students who were sixth graders in 2003–2004 and seventh graders in 2004–2005) consisted of 125 students. Group Two (students who were seventh graders in 2003–2004 and eighth graders in 2004–2005) consisted of 154 students. (Thom, 2006, p. 53)

UNIT OF ANALYSIS

The unit of analysis is the "who" or "what" the researcher is studying. The study may a single person, small group, larger entity such as a school district or business, artifacts, geographical units, or other forms of aggregated data (Trochim, 2006). The unit of analysis is related to the study's research questions/hypotheses and sets boundaries for the study (Patton, 2002; Yin, 2003b).

Examples

- An important step in research design is to determine the unit of analysis—or the unit about which statements are being made. In this study, proposed theory, data collection and statistical analyses were conducted at the organizational level. Therefore, the unit of analysis for this study was the individual agency. (Akbulut, 2003, p. 48)
- The sixth goal was to test the presumption that cohesion and discrepancy reduction mechanisms interact to increase the congruence between the value system and part-time work experiences, or in other words, increase consistency within the

person-in-context unit of analysis forwarded within the developmental-contextual meta model of human development. Finally, the seventh goal was to examine whether the cohesion and discrepancy reduction mechanisms promoting harmony between work values and experience varied as a function of person- and context-level variability. (Porfeli, 2004, pp. 251–52)

RESEARCH VARIABLES

In this section, the researcher describes the research variables the researcher intends to use in the study, as well as the attributes associated with each of the variables. "Attributes are characteristics or qualities that describe an object. . . . Anything you might say to describe yourself or someone else involves an attribute" (Babbie, 2001, p. 17). The researcher describes the independent, dependent, and any confounding or extraneous variables that are part of the study (Heffner, 2004a).

Examples

- Based on the research questions and hypothesis identified for this study, several dependent, independent, and control variables have been identified. Further details of the dependent, independent, and control variables are discussed in the following sections of this document. . . . The dependent variables in this study were the perceptions of student-to-student interaction, teacher-to-student interactions, and student satisfaction. Both of the variables, student-to-student and student-to-teacher interaction, were measured independently by summing the responses to each of the questions identified on the perception of interaction. . . . The primary independent variables investigated were learning strategies, student-to-student interaction, and student-to-teacher interaction. (Bailey, 2002, pp. 44–45)
- The dependent variable in this study was the stakeholders' perceived level of satisfaction with the economic development strategies employed by the community colleges in their service area. The independent variables used in this study were categorized into two groups: the personal factors of the respondents and the institutional factors of the community col-

leges within the geographic region of the study. (Gossett, 2002, p. 87)

RESEARCH INSTRUMENT

This section provides the reader with a complete description of the research instrument used to collect data. A research instrument's purpose is to measure the study's variable(s) and other pertinent data (Pierce, 2009). The researcher describes each instrument with appropriate cited references as well as the instrument's validity and reliability. The researcher includes references to other substantive research in appropriately related fields where the instruments were used to collect similar data.

Examples

- A demographic questionnaire was devised that includes questions regarding general demographic information, (i.e., age, gender, marital status, grade, major, ethnicity). This instrument is found in Appendix C. (Nicolas, 2002, p. 36)
- Beck Depressioň Inventory (BDI). The BDI (Beck, 1978) is a self-report measure designed to assess for severity of depression, with an emphasis on its cognitive, affective, and behavioral symptoms. Presence of somatic symptoms is not emphasized, with only one such symptom measured (fatigue). The BDI employs a four-point Likert-type scale (0–3) wherein 0 = absence of symptoms, 1 = mild symptom, 2 = moderate, and 3 = severe or debilitating symptom. For the present study, the total BDI score was utilized, with a range of 0 to 63 total score (a score of 15 or higher indicating clinically elevated level of depressive symptoms). (Gaines, 2001, p. 25)
- Multiple items were proposed to measure each latent construct in this study (see Figure 3). It is customary for squares in models to represent observed variables and circles to represent latent variables. Each construct is described below following the demographic questionnaire. (House, 2004, p. 57)
- This study had two phases: (1) identifying instructional elements existing in the sample, and (2) rating courses using these elements. Identifying course elements involved a literature review spanning traditional and distance education. Notable design elements were recorded in a "descriptors list" that

serves as the theoretical basis for an instrument (necessary to complete the second research phase). This list led to a pilot study involving nine courses from five online high schools. School selection was based on school reputation, age, size, offerings, student types, and willingness to participate. Course selection included biased randomization, ensuring inclusion of all schools and subjects. Because courses were the unit of analysis, human subjects protocols were unnecessary. (Keeler, 2003, p. 1)

PILOT STUDY

The term pilot study refers to a small-scale version, or trial run, to test or assess a research instrument as a precursor to a more general study. A pilot study may work as a fail-safe measure to identify the instrument's limitations (van Teijlingen and Hundley, 2001). Moreover, the researcher can use the data from the pilot study to modify the research design and data collection instruments and protocols. The researcher describes the demographic makeup of the pilot group and the conditions under which the group piloted the instrument (International University of Professional Studies, 2004).

Examples

- The questionnaire design was piloted before its distribution. Copies of two proposed questionnaires were sent to ten current or former superintendents who were selected because of their knowledge and expertise regarding district finance. They were asked to review the proposed document for clarity of instructions, preference for design, face validity, and other constructive suggestions to improve the survey design. The suggestions gathered from this process were considered in the final design decisions. (Neill, 2003, p. 29)
- Once the researcher gained a preliminary understanding of PECS effectiveness from the observations, this information was then used to develop pilot surveys for parents and teachers of children with autism who had been taught PECS. After developing the pilot surveys, the researcher collaborated with parents and teachers in guided interviews to fine-tune the survey items ensuring that the surveys were consumer friendly

and would result in maximally useful information. (Greenberg, 2011 p. 59)

DATA COLLECTION PROCEDURES

In this section, the researcher identifies the plan for collecting data indicating the type of data needed to answer the research questions/ hypotheses and identify the use of equipment or other types of supplies in the data gathering procedures. The researcher also identifies tests, surveys, data-gathering sites, record-keeping procedures, and how the data-gathering methods are organized. In general, this section comprises four parts: design, participants, instruments, and procedures (Wong, 2002).

Examples

- The data were collected with a survey developed for this study and distributed to mental health practitioners in a 12-county region of Southeast Ohio. The survey responses are presented, including descriptive data incorporating both demographic information and the exploration of issues discussed in the retention literature. Three-hundred-and-twenty surveys were sent out: 60 to one mental health center, 30 to another (together they covered six rural counties), and 230 that were randomly chosen from a list of individuals described in Chapter III. Out of the 60 surveys sent to the first mental health agency surveys, 45 (75 percent) were returned. The second agency returned 24 of 30 (80 percent). Of the 230 mailed surveys, 98 (43 percent) were returned. Twenty-two surveys were returned because the individuals moved. Overall, 163 (51 percent) usable surveys were returned. (Meyer, 2003, p. 88)
- Attendance information for the current study was obtained through a retrospective review of the participants' medical records. Baseline data collection occurred between 1992 and 1995. Volunteers were consecutively recruited during their initial appointments with the HIV outpatient clinic. Participants included individuals who had been diagnosed with HIV and were receiving outpatient medical treatment at the above-mentioned clinic (EKL). Informed consent was obtained prior to participation in the study (see Appendix D). Demographic

information was obtained from patient interviews conducted during the initial clinic appointment and from the baseline demographics questionnaire completed by patients. Information concerning disease status and other medical information was obtained through a review of the patients' medical records at baseline. Participants were paid five dollars for completion of the baseline questionnaires. Following baseline data collection all scheduled clinic appointments, including physician and nurse visits, were monitored via chart reviews for a period of three years from the patient's entry into the study. Appointment attendance information (frequency of scheduled, canceled, and "no show" appointments) was obtained from a retrospective review of the patients' medical records. When available, other important information such as changes in attending physician and reason for discharge from the clinic (e.g. deceased, relocating) was also recorded during examination of the patients' medical records. (D. M. Johnson, 2002, pp. 21–22)

DATA COLLECTION AND STATISTICAL ANALYSIS

In this section, the researcher describes how data were collected, reported, and analyzed. The researcher lists methods, software, statistical procedures, or qualitative content analysis methods used in the data analysis.

Data analysis has three components: data preparation, a description of the population, and analysis (Trochim, 2006). The researcher cites the use of statistical software programs such as SPSS, NUD*IST, or other programs, providing an explanation as to how they were used in the data analysis.

Examples

• I used a constant comparative method of data analysis. As I indicated earlier, I audio tape–recorded interviews with participants and had the interviews transcribed verbatim. Analysis of data began with the transcriptions. I made analytic memos as the transcription proceeded. I read the transcriptions and coded them immediately after each transcription. As I coded the data, I looked for relationships and patterns and attempted to fit them into categories. After I collected and transcribed all data, I reread the transcriptions comparing the responses of all of the participants that I interviewed. I searched for similarities and differences in key words or phrases, time, relationships, feelings and perceptions. I analyzed concepts for how and why the participants perceive school now, as well as how and why they performed as they did while they were students. I recoded and re-categorized as new concepts emerged. As themes emerged, I began to interpret the data and developed theories. I stored data on note cards in file boxes by themes. I made copies of transcriptions to preserve the original, and conducted coding and recoding, cutting and pasting on copies. I stored and labeled tapes by dates and participant code names. (Carper, 2002, p. 45)

- An analysis of documents and existing scholarship provided information about international and national level notions and practices with regard to community schools in Mali (See Appendix A). These documents (including agency and donor reports, monitoring and evaluation materials, specific program documents on community schools from SC/USA, Ministry of Education documents) revealed factors that helped shape perceptions of community schools at international and national levels in particular. At the international level, existing scholarship that addressed community schools or similar education strategies outside of the formal system was identified for a literature review. (Capacci-Carneal, 2004, p. 30)
- For the handgrip task a repeated measures (RM) multivariate analysis of variance (MANOVA) was employed with gender as a between subjects factor, and time intervals (15 sec) nested within three sensation variables nested within three clusters (i.e., physical, motivational and affective sensations) as repeated factors and gender as a between subjects factor. For the cycle task a RMMANOVA was employed with time intervals (30 sec) nested within three sensation variables as repeated factors and gender as a between subjects factor. A hierarchical linear regression analysis was conducted to determine how much of the variance in "time to fatigue" was accounted for by dispositional and task-specific factors. The significance level used in this study was $p \leq 0.05$. (Hutchinson, 2004, p. 29)

SETTING AND ENVIRONMENT

The researcher provides a rich and detailed description of the setting and environment in which the study was conducted. In describing the setting, the researcher describes the study's context, identifying appropriate members within the context, and other internal or external forces influencing the study (Baron, 2005).

Examples

- The first half of my study occurred in an urban elementary school, Frost Elementary, situated in the southeastern part of the United States. This school was chosen mainly for its diverse student population. Other factors considered were the constructivist philosophy espoused by staff, the organizational structure that allows students to change classes for certain subjects, and its small number of students. Approximately 500 students attend the school from 9:00 am until 3:30 pm. It is designated a gifted and talented magnet elementary school. The designation of magnet school means Frost Elementary draws students from the western and southern parts of the county to complement the students who are assigned from a base area around the inner-city school. Magnet students travel up to one hour each way on a school bus or by car to get to the school. (Godfrey, 2003, p. 81)
- Setting and Recruitment: A large teaching hospital located in the southeastern United States was the recruitment site for the larger parent study. Participants were recruited by core team members of the parent study either in the kidney transplant clinic or at various renal dialysis clinics. The participants signed consent forms after a thorough explanation by core team members. Following approval by the university's Institutional Review Board the principal investigator of the parent study provided de-identified data and the secondary data analysis was conducted. (Cupples, 2010, p. 34)

BIAS AND ERROR

Quick Tip: Research integrity is essential. Acknowledging bias and error may mitigate how some interpret the importance of the study; yet, the acknowledgment of any bias and/or error increases the researcher's cred ibility and integrity.

In this section, the researcher acknowledges potential bias and error that occurred leading to and during the study. The researcher indicates the sources of bias, conditions, or circumstances that affected the study's validity. Reporting the bias or error, or the potential for the existence for bias and error, substantiates the conclusions the researcher draws from the data analysis.

According to Sica (2006), "Bias is a form of systematic error [with] innumerable causes. . . . Bias can be related to . . . the method in which study variables are collected or measured, the attitudes or preferences of an investigator, and lack of control of confounding variables."

Example

- One of the advantages of a participant-observer approach is that the researcher enters into the world of her/his informants and is able to describe the complex system of social interactions. This provided the researcher with more of an insider's view of the situation being studied, helping to validate his/her findings. This same advantage can be construed as a situation that might encourage bias in the researchers' reporting of data and so must be balanced with controls. Use of collaborative teacher-researcher provides an insider who can challenge the interpretations of the researcher. A constant check for rival hypotheses or negative instances also provides control. The use of value free note taking with separate personal and analytical notes provides a more unbiased approach. (Mather, 2004, p. 79)

VALIDITY

In this section, the researcher reports how the study meets the rigorous standards of validity. "Validity refers to the accuracy or truthfulness of a measurement" (Walonick, 2004, chap. 3, Validity and Reliability section, para. 2). Regardless of research methodology, the researcher addresses the various types of validity pertinent to the study.

There are four types of validity: conclusion validity, internal validity, construct validity, and external validity (Trochim, 2006). Qualitative researchers, for example, may describe *triangulation, member checking, repeated observations, peer scrutiny of the data,* and *collaboration within the research* as a way of showing the study's validity (Merriam, 2001).

Examples

- McCubbin et al. (2001) described validity evaluations using the CHIP subscales with a sample of families raising children diagnosed with cerebral palsy. The results documented that the utilization of all three coping patterns was greatest among mothers and fathers living in families with higher conflict (McCubbin et al., 2001). McCubbin et al. (1983) used the CHIP to measure parental coping with children diagnosed with cystic fibrosis (CF). The construct validity of CHIP was evaluated utilizing the Family Environment Scale (FES; Moos and Moos, 1976) and height/weight and pulmonary function indexes of the child with CF (McCubbin et al., 1983). The purpose of the FES development was to examine specific features of a family, which included social and environment (Moos and Moos, 1976). (Hall, 2008, p. 37)
- Due to the nature of qualitative research, many researchers have argued that the term validity is not applicable. For this study, I will refer to the concept of traditional validity within quantitative formulas as "trustworthy," "relevant," "credible" or seventy-five "representative" research outcomes. Thus, in qualitative research the most basic aspect of validity centers on how representative the results are and how justifiable the findings become (Winter, 2000). I will use the following methods to find a greater sense of trustworthiness and credibility in my research: Negative Case Analysis, Member Checks, Panel of Experts, and Outside Researcher Review. By employing these tools, I intend to establish relevant research in relation to the questions proposed. Recently, Becker detailed an alternative approach to validity criteria, utilizing the tenets of accuracy, precision and breadth (in press). All these items re-

late to the need for prolonged, rigorous engagement with the subject matter. (Farrell, 2006, 74–75)

TRUSTWORTHINESS

Qualitative researchers provide a rationale for the trustworthiness of their data. The researcher provides evidence for trustworthiness by triangulating the data to make claims for the data's credibility, transferability, dependability, and confirmability (Guba and Lincoln, 1981). Some studies require multiple measures and observations; the researcher provides evidence that the data have been triangulated as a means of ensuring the validity of the study.

Triangulation is a qualitative process testing the consistency of findings harvested through different methods and sources of data, including field notes, artifacts, and transcripts (Trochim, 2006).

Example

- Lincoln and Guba (1985) proposed four alternative constructs to ensure the validity of qualitative data analysis (i.e., credibility, transferability, dependability, confirmability). The researcher addressed all four of these constructs by providing the reader with a detailed description of the procedures and results for both credibility and dependability. In addition, the researcher listened to the participants with an empathic ear in order not to bias the conversations. The transferability of this research was not an issue. This study was conducted to reflect services and professionals in Iowa but the same procedures could be used in other states or with other disability populations (i.e., deaf/hard of hearing). (Blankenship, 2004, p. 128)

RELIABILITY

Reliability indicates the study's ability to be replicated and produce similar results (Heffner, 2004b). When measuring reliability, the researcher provides evidence that the instruments produce consistent results over time as well as identifying the various methods used to test reliability (Walonick, 2004).

Examples

- In designing the study, the author planned ahead to verify results, recognizing that "reliability and validity should not be evaluated at the end of the project, but should be goals that shape the entire research process, influencing study design, data collection, and analysis choices" (Cohen and Crabtree, 2008). However, like methodology, quality in qualitative research often becomes entangled in larger discourses of ontology and epistemology (Pope and Mays, 2006, p. 90). Like many other aspects of qualitative research, the proper way to verify results is subject to controversy and grounded in entrenched philosophy. Mays and Pope (2000) suggest two main schools of thought for qualitative research in health care. The first one states that validity and reliability, as defined by the realist paradigm, are important criteria for evaluating qualitative research; without them, qualitative research risks being seen as unscientific and inexact. The second states that applying empirical standards of validity and reliability to qualitative research is inappropriate, and therefore qualitative researchers must define their own standards for quality. (Dejoy, 2011, pp. 81–82)
- The embedded case study protocols are described in the data collection process. The case study protocols include the rules and guidelines for the data gathering process (Yin, 1994). Three methods were employed to maintain reliability: (1) The researcher recognized the potential for inherent bias as an employee and researcher in USD 411 (Bogdan and Biklen, 1998). To control for this, the researcher's position was clearly stated to participants as both researcher and employee of USD 411. (2) Using the constant comparative method, the data were triangulated between collection methods, comparing data between and within themes. (3) A rich and detailed description of the methodology was recorded for an audit trail (Merriam, 2001). The study's reliability was further enhanced through consistency in the questions asked for all focus groups and interviews. (Fast, 2005, p. 46)

SUMMARY

In many dissertations, there is a summary or conclusion section at the end of chapter 3. Here the researcher describes the salient points covered in chapter 3. At the conclusion of the summary the researcher provides a brief summary of what the reader can expect in the next chapter.

Examples

- This chapter first situated my study within the framework of ethnographic inquiry, which seeks to document the cosmology of a culture (Bishop, 1999, p. 3). In light of the deterritorialized nature of the subject of my study (or that of any other ethnographic fieldworks in this globalized world), I further presented Appadurai's (1991, 1996) cosmopolitan ethnograph, a methodology that embraces a global approach in addition to the traditional localizing strategy employed by ethnographers. After addressing my position as a native ethnographer, the methodological discussion centered around a detailed account of my ethnographic field/homework as well as the problematics that emerged in the process. The next chapter explores mediascapes during the 2001 Spring Festival. (Ren, 2003, p. 81)
- This chapter focused on the organization, inspiration and methodology which informs the process of inquiry that underpins this work (see Figure 1). It is best represented as a synergistic confluence of thought that integrates three central ideas: a body of writing can take the form of a woven tapestry; different contemporary thinkers and philosophers profoundly informed and inspired the creation of this project from its inception; and qualitative research methodologies sometimes converge to serve as an epistemological framework for philosophical inquiry. (Cooper, 2002, p. 47)

Pep Talk

A traditional dissertation is comprised of five chapters. At this point, the researcher is more than halfway to the finish line.

Great things are done by a series of small things brought together.
—Vincent van Gogh

FOUR

Results/Findings

Chapter 4 is the results/finding chapter (the use of terms "results" or "findings" depends on the study's methodology). Quantitative researchers use the term "results" and qualitative researchers use the term "findings." The form for writing the results chapter can differ. Some departments tie results and discussion together. Others require reporting results in scholarly journal format. The purpose of the chapter is to accurately and ethically report the importance and credibility of each result (Patton, 2002). The chapter concludes with a summarization of data and a preview of the forthcoming chapter.

The following components are commonly found in chapter 4:

- Introduction
- Organizing the Results/Findings Chapter
- Methodology Summary
- Population, Sample, and Participants
- Results/Findings
- Summary of Results/Findings
- Summary and Transition to Chapter 5

Note: Always consult with your academic department and advisor for the required contents for your discipline

---

Quick Tip: Many dissertations provide a quick overview of the study's purpose, problem statement, research questions, and methodology. Copy and paste these sections from chapter 1 or chapter 3 to ensure accuracy.

INTRODUCTION

Chapter 4 begins with an introduction that states the purpose of the chapter. Depending on departmental norms, the chapter's purpose may be followed by a succinct summary of the chapter's organization.

Examples

- Chapter IV presents the results from this study. Results are presented in three sections. The first contains information about the empirical sampling distributions of the fit statistics. . . . The second section contains results that relate to the prediction of the scaling corrections. Included are summaries of the multilevel models that were fitted to the data. . . . The third section presents results that relate to the application of the prediction equations to real items. (Hanson, 2004, p. 103)
- Five central themes were identified by this study to be common in meaningful learning experiences: (a) risk, (b) awkwardness, (c) fractional sublimation, (d) reconstruction, and (e) growth. . . . The themes and their respective attributes are substantiated by the writings and comments from this study's participants. Some examples of participants' statements are given in this chapter to illustrate their perspectives, and additional examples from the participants can be found in Appendix G under the themes and attributes they represent. (Taniguchi, 2004, p. 79)
- The previous chapter described the study design and methodology applied in this dissertation for selecting the study sample, linking the methodology to the research questions for the study, matching the measures employed to the study constructs, and testing the strength and nature of the relationship between constructs. . . . Section 5.1 discusses the factor analysis findings of the dissertation in three stages. . . . Stage 2 analyzes the comprehensive factor analysis results for the longitudinal data, controls for and compares these results to conceptual expectations and the yearly panel results. . . . The complete data results from the factor analyses conducted in Stages 1 through 3 are listed in Appendix A." (Adams, 2004, p. 38)

ORGANIZATION OF THE STUDY'S RESULTS/FINDINGS

> Quick Tip: Above all—be ethical, act with integrity—objectivity is central.

Begin with a clear and logical plan to present the results concisely, accurately, and understandably. There are multiple ways to organize results into an understandable format. Researchers commonly use charts, figures, graphs, and tables as organizational markers. In fields emphasizing quantitative research, it is common to organize the reporting of results by hypotheses, restating each hypothesis and addressing each hypothesis as a separate subheading in the same order as presented in chapter 1 (Poland, 2003). In qualitative research, it is common to organize by patterns that emerge from data analysis. The researcher includes a section on the differences discovered in the patterns emerging from the data, indicating how the patterns support or do not support the research questions (Berkowitz, 1997). In fields emphasizing quantitative research, the findings may be organized by hypothesis, experiment, or other organizational schema (Burnard, 2004). Summarize the results/findings at the end of each subsection and again at the end of the chapter 4.

Examples

- The aim of this analysis is to evaluate the current situation in terms of computer technology integration in Cyprus elementary schools. In particular through data analysis the study attempts to identify how elementary teachers in Cyprus apply computers in their classroom practices. Moreover, the study attempts to identify the factors that influence teachers in using computer technology in the classroom. The quantitative analysis presented in this chapter includes descriptive and inferential statistics. Version 11 of the SPSS statistical package was used to analyze the quantitative data. (Eteokleous, 2004, p. 41)
- The results are presented in two major sections. The first represents the analyses that test the general causal model (see Figure 1). Within this section, path analysis methods are used to test the hypotheses that age only indirectly affects information search and quality of decision rationale through its influence on working memory, vocabulary, preference for control in health decision making, and prior knowledge of cancer di-

agnosis and treatment. Also in this section is a presentation of a model that has been optimized for the data. (Talbot, 2004, p. 49)

- In this chapter, I begin with a description of the sample, and I present the data from their responses arranged by instrument. I am starting with a description of the sample because it is often assumed that the audience for museum theatre is exclusively children, but as can be seen in the sample, spectators were a diverse group in terms of age. I have analyzed data through both quantitative and qualitative methods, and I approach findings from the quantitative data before the qualitative in order to first show statistical results are then teased out in participants. (Hughes, 2008, p. 137)

METHODOLOGY SUMMARY

In this section, the researcher summarizes the methodology, making sure the summary is consistent with what was previously reported in chapters 1 and 3.

Examples

- This study began in February 2002, with a convenience sample of five classrooms whose teachers volunteered to be a part of the study. The heterogeneous classrooms are located in two elementary schools in the same school district. The school district is located seventy miles north-northwest of New York City. A naturalistic approach was taken by gathering information through classroom observations and by sharing with the teachers after each observation the information that was gathered. Quantitative data were obtained from the Grade-4 Science Program Evaluation Test (PET). Data were collected on-site at three different times. Data found on the Classroom Spatial Utilization Form and a map of each classroom was prepared while visiting each classroom after regular school hours. Classroom observations were conducted during March and April to collect data recorded on the Classroom Migration Form. The Grade-4 Science PET was administered in May 2002. (Duncanson, 2003, p. 109)
- In the first experiment, it was shown that articulatory suppression effects are differentiated from irrelevant sound ef-

fects (speech and non-speech) according to the influence they have on neural processing during a working memory task. An intriguing aspect of the time course data was that these differences appeared at distinct stages of the trial, with articulatory suppression effects emerging within the working memory network very early in the trial (during encoding), and irrelevant sound effects emerging later in the trial (as delay-based processing sets in). These temporal differences suggest a novel behavioral method for dissociating the effects of suppression and irrelevant sound by manipulating the specific timing of irrelevant information during the trial (e.g., by limiting irrelevant information to encoding only, delay only, or retrieval only). Accordingly, the main goal of the second experiment was to explore whether articulatory suppression and irrelevant sounds have different consequences for behavior when limited temporally to a particular stage of the working memory task trial. (Chein, 2004, p. 56)

POPULATION, SAMPLE, AND PARTICIPANTS

If the researcher uses human subjects, the researcher describes the subjects, the source of the subject pool, the selection process, number of subjects, and criteria for selection (Columbia University School of Nursing, 2003). This section is followed by a report of the results/findings (Baron, 2005).

Example

- Research hypothesis 2: The students' perceptions of feedback effectiveness, as reflected by their scores on the Feedback Effectiveness Survey (Appendix E, page 169), are significantly higher during the intervention periods, B1 and B2, than during the baseline periods, A1 and A2. A General Linear Model Repeated Measures procedure reflects temporal differences (á = .05). The univariate test for period-related differences on the dependent variable Feedback Effect (Table 4) provided disconfirming results; contrary to Hypothesis 2, the means of the Feedback Effect did not significantly vary by period. (Waddell, 2004, p. 85)

RESULTS/FINDINGS

> **Quick Tip:** *Results* report quantitative studies. *Findings* report qualitative studies.

In this section the researcher presents the study's results/findings. The researcher aligns the results/findings to the research questions or hypotheses. They are reported accurately without interpretation, guided by a strong understanding of research ethics. The results/findings are reported consistent with the norms of the researcher's discipline and academic department. Some disciplines, for example, may require the use of the American Psychological Association (2010) guidelines, while other disciplines may require use of the *Chicago Manual of Style 16th Edition* (University of Chicago Press, 2010). The length of the results/findings section varies according to the research design and methodological approach.

The researcher, if using quantitative methods, describes the data and the treatment of the data. The researcher reports the data in sufficient detail to justify any conclusions, often adding charts, figures, and tables. If the researcher uses qualitative methods, Miles and Huberman (1994) suggest results be presented using descriptive and organized text associated with graphic organizers such as matrices.

Examples

- The results from the adult hobbyists suggested that there were some patterns that might be useful in classrooms, but I suspected that adults might have different types of satisfactions than do high school students. The school culture could also affect the kinds of satisfactions that students take from their work and play. Another concern with the first survey was the possibility that something in the wording of the examples skewed the results. To eliminate these concerns a revised survey for high school students used examples drawn from hobbyists' comments on the previous survey. The extrinsic motivator, "Be better than others," included this example: "Off road motorcycle riding—I hate to admit it, but yes I do really like that I am good at riding, better than most others. It does add to my enjoyment." (Pfaffman, 2003, p. 22)

- Statistical analyses: Due to the exploratory nature of the first study, power analyses were not conducted to determine sample sizes required to detect differences in mean outcome evaluations of the two message frames used to present arguments for Ariva® use by smokers or the product evaluations. The self-reported baseline characteristics of participants in each group were compared. Means + the standard error of the mean (SEM) are reported. Discrete variables were analyzed using the chi-square test of Fischer's exact test. Continuous variables were analyzed using a two-sample test, or the Wilcoxon rank sum test where assumptions of normality were violated. Tests were two-tailed and a significance level of 0.05 alpha or less was used. (Edwards, 2007, p. 35)

SUMMARY OF RESULTS/FINDINGS

In this section, the researcher presents an overall summary of the results/findings, conveying to the reader the salient results/findings.

Examples

- Here is a summary of OCAI findings across unique subcultures: HQMUSE (university headquarters) OCAI data (n = 19 returned surveys with good data of 38 mailed or 50 percent return rate) reveals a dominant hierarchy type. The aggregate scores for each "now" and "preferred" culture types were: clan (26/36); adhocracy (14/17); market (27/27); and hierarchy (32/27). This was the only subculture of the sixteen examined that rated adhocracy as the lowest type in both now and preferred categories. In addition, this was the only subunit that rated hierarchy as both present and somewhat desirable (statistically significant, p <.05). All of the other subunits rated hierarchy as least preferred. (Paparone, 2003, p. 90)
- In conclusion, aggregate analyses of the final sample data provided some significant results that will in turn assist in the further understanding of the pharmacist-patient relationship. An exploratory common factor analysis was useful in analyzing survey item 2 in order to answer RQ1. Three primary pharmacist roles were identified: (1) traditional role, (2) health care provider role, and (3) alternative therapy source role. Key characteristics and expectations inherent in each role were

also noted according to the strength of their loadings. Survey item 7 was examined via correlation analyses and independent samples T-tests in order to explore RQ2. While more research will be necessary in order to fully understand the influence safety issues may have on pharmacist-patient interactions, both respondent groups agreed upon the basic premise that patients should talk to health care providers when experiencing difficulties with medications and/or new therapies. Finally, frequencies were calculated on survey item 9 to explore the perceived credibility of various health information sources and technologies as questions by RQ3. As expected, pharmacists were perceived to be credible information sources whereas the Internet is questionable, according to patient responses. Overall, further research will be necessary in order to adequately assess RQ2 and RQ3. (Gade, 2003, p. 61)

CHAPTER SUMMARY AND TRANSITION TO CHAPTER 5

In some dissertations, the researcher summarizes the results as above and includes a transition to chapter 5.

Examples

- In summary, this chapter described some of the participants' experiences within the Youth Partnership Project. The data analysis provided insight to the participants' experiences through their understanding of the project and its process, participants' perspective of their experiences within the project, strategies used within the project, and meaning developed from their experiences within the project. The questions that guided the study were the following: (1) How do youth and adults who are engaged in developing a sustainable development plan describe their experience within the process of the project? (2) What role does the implementation of a collaborative method play in enhancing civic engagement involving both youth and adults, if any? The final chapter will address the above questions that assisted me in exploring elements within the process of civic engagement. The chapter will also speak to insights constructed from the literature review, as well as contributions of the study and possible future research needs based on the findings of the study or information notfound within the study. (Reno, 2003, pp. 95–96)

- In this chapter, results from quantitative analyses were presented for the two research questions. For each dimension of both instruments, teachers' mean score was above the midpoint of the Likert-type response scales indicating that respondents tended to perceive their school as moving in the direction of a PLC and that respondents tended to report moderate to strong teachers' self-efficacy beliefs. The dimensions of the two instruments were, for the most part, moderately to strongly related, but negatively so. In addition, several, but not all, of the correlations were statistically significant. Finally, schools assigned to high and low scoring groups based on means calculated for SPSLCQ did not differ statistically on the dimensions of teachers' self-efficacy beliefs. Chapter 5 presents a discussion of the results as well as conclusions and implications of the findings. The study will conclude with recommendations for future research. (Nolan, 2009, p. 72)

Pep Talk

The researcher sees the summit of the dissertation mountain. It's a short journey to reach the top. The researcher pushes on with a sense of urgency while visualizing being caped by the advisor.

Great things are done when men [women] and mountains meet.
—William Blake

FIVE

Interpretation and Recommendations

In chapter 5, the researcher provides the reader with an interpretation of the results/findings; the relationship of the results/findings to the research questions or hypotheses; the relationship of the results/findings to relevant theory or praxis; an analysis of the strengths and limitations of the study; and recommendations for future research, offering a rationale why the study is an important contribution to new knowledge and how it advances practice.

The following components are often found in chapter 5:

- Introduction
- Summary of Results
- Discussion of Results
- Summary Statement
- Implications for Further Research
- Implications for Practice and Recommendations
- Relationship of Results to Theory
- Limitations
- Summary and Conclusion

Note: Always consult with your academic department and advisor for the required contents for your discipline.

> **Quick Tip:** Chapter 5 represents the gestalt of the dissertation learning process. Bring together the wisdom, knowledge, and insights gained in the dissertation process in this chapter.

INTRODUCTION

In the introduction, briefly restate

- The purpose of the study
- The problem statement
- The research questions or hypotheses
- The salient theoretical perspectives
- The methodology
- The results

> **Quick Tip:** Copy and paste the summaries of the purpose of the study, problem statement, research questions or hypotheses, salient theoretical perspectives, and methodology from chapter 3. Remember—maintain ab solute consistency between all chapters.

Examples

- Chapter One of this work situates the context in which the study was implemented. In addition to positioning this study in the crossroads of political, social, and economic dilemmas . . . Chapter Two of this work addresses the review of literature. This researcher acknowledges that there is a dearth of research that explicitly examines the perspectives of school board members' views on engagement with private charitable foundations. . . . Chapter Three of this work details the research methodology employed within this study. . . . Chapter Four of this work presents the findings of this study. The findings are organized by each of the study's four research questions, whereas the questions situate the subjects' thoughts on perspectives, practices, problems, and prospects given public-private partnerships (Acar, 2001). . . . Chapter Five discusses the major and minor findings associated with this study. (Palmiero, 2011, pp. 173–74).
- This chapter highlights the major findings from this study of principals' perceptions of the implementation of the instruc-

tional leadership program, Skillful Observation and Coaching Laboratory (SOCL), in one rural county. This chapter will also address theoretical and practical implications from the study and specify limitations. The chapter concludes with recommendations for future research on the implementation of SOCL or other instructional leadership professional development programs. (Carraway, 2012, p. 117)

- As described in Chapter 1, I designed this research project to begin identifying the components of teacher interest and to explore how teacher interest affects student interest in a subject. By examining the interaction between teacher interest and student subject interest in two core subjects (social studies and English) where student attendance was required, I focused on the teacher's role in influencing student subject interest. This information was especially important because a relationship of interest represents positive value for the person who is pursuing the object. Therefore, teachers and students who actively pursue a subject of interest can expect to derive benefit from their connections with the subject. The research questions developed to explore the process of connecting with the content are restated below. (Long, 2003, p. 157)

SUMMARY OF RESULTS/FINDINGS

In this section, the researcher summarizes the results/findings identified in chapter 4. The researcher may list the results/findings as a group and then discuss each separately, or list a single result/finding, discuss it, and repeat the process for each of the remaining results.

Examples

- The present study focused on questions regarding ethnicity, level of religiosity, remorse, and forgiveness. Analyses related to hypothesis one examined possible ethnicity differences for all major variables. As expected, there were differences found among African Americans and Caucasians related to religiosity, providing support for the first hypothesis. Here, African Americans tended to report higher levels of religiosity (partner) than their Caucasian counterparts and that they attended religious services more often during the past year than did Caucasians (self and partner). This is not surprising given past research that reports that African Americans have a strong religious orientation overall and tend to be more religious than the general population (Taylor, Chatters, Jayakody, and Levin, 1996). (Bedell, 2002, p. 76)

- No support emerged from the current study for any of our four hypotheses. First, the study provided no support for the hypothesis that overly positive self-perceptions and aggressive behavior would be positively associated cross-sectionally. Second, the study provided no support for the hypothesis that the relation between overly positive self-perceptions and aggression increases as children progress through adolescence. Third, the results provided no support for the hypothesis that overly positive self-perceptions predict later aggressive behavior. Finally, the results of the current study provided no support for the notion that aggressive behavior predicts later levels of overly positive self-perceptions. (Hoffman, 2003, p. 44)

DISCUSSION OF RESULTS/FINDINGS

In the discussion section, the researcher provides a rationale for interpreting the results/findings and drawing conclusions. In doing so, the researcher offers personal insights and links these insights to the relevant literature examined in chapter 2, the "Review of the Literature."

Here the researcher introduces the Discussion of Results/Findings, by stating something like, "This section provides a summary of the results used to address the five research questions of this study. The results are summarized after each of the listed research question below" (Hoare, 2007, p. 113).

In the examples that follow, the researchers discuss their results/findings.

Examples

- The previous two chapters detail and analyze data gathered in this research study. In this concluding chapter I reflect on the implications of these findings. More specifically, I consider ways in which Ontario's special education identification, placement, and program delivery model might be restructured with the aim of fostering a dynamic that is more transparent and inclusive. In the initial sections of the chapter I explain why a shift in policy is needed, by outlining how I conceptualize special education in Ontario as something that exists on an inclusion/exclusion and transparency/opaqueness continuum (see Table 3). In the latter segments of the chapter I outline a complex network of policy pathways (see Figure 3) along with their associated repercussions. This discussion chapter is divided into the following five sections: The Inclusion/Exclusion, Transparency/Opaqueness Continuum; Policy Pathways; Policy Complications; Implications of Study; and Conclusion. (Cobb, 2010, p. 174)

- The implications of this study's findings are important for families, schools, and larger communities. Millions of dollars are being spent each year trying to determine the root causes and cures for social ills, yet with seemingly little success in many cases. I believe that our continued failures at societal reform are the result of the same "bigger and better" approach noted by Torrance (1979) in which "new" solutions are not really new, they are simply bigger and more expensive versions of the same tired schemes that have always failed before. (Kyzer, 2001, 245–46)

SUMMARY STATEMENT

The summary statement summarizes the results/findings and draws conclusions. The researcher, when using a conclusion section at the end of the entire discussion section, restates the significance of the study and raises new questions generated from the research (Brown, 1997).

Examples

- In summary, even though many Egyptian preservice teachers expressed a willingness to teach students with special needs in their classrooms, they did not necessarily feel prepared to teach in inclusive settings. Pre- and in-service training was seen as an important factor in improving their attitudes and feelings of preparedness to teach in inclusive settings. Participants in this study considered their current level of training as inadequate simply because they did not know how to help students with special needs in general education classrooms. Perhaps the most discouraging finding was that not a single participant mentioned curricular adaptations or instructional techniques as a reason for being willing to teach students with special needs. Preservice teachers who expressed their willingness to teach students with special needs in their classrooms attributed their disposition to personal characteristics and experiences unrelated to their preparation in the teacher education program. (El-Ashry, 2009, p. 108)

• This study represents one of the most comprehensive to date, measuring agreement, using multiple methods, among more than 38,000 incumbents in 61 occupational series and 261 series grades. As predicted, agreement failed to reach acceptable levels in nearly every case. However, contrary to expectation, experience, occupational complexity, and KSAO abstractness accounted for little of the disagreement. Although the reasons for these null findings are not entirely clear, the most likely explanation is that true cross-position variance simply overshadowed the variance due to these rater, occupation, and item characteristics. If so, then the disagreement reported here reflects a coarse classification system that inadequately distinguishes among meaningful subgroups within single occupational titles. The existence of such subgroups threatens not so much the predictive validity of job specifications as their content validity, insofar as predictive KSAOs are not identified as such. Future research must focus on the existence of such subgroups, their consequences, and ways of identifying them. (Bumkrant, 2003, p. 74)

IMPLICATIONS FOR FURTHER RESEARCH

Quick Tip: Imagine taking this study forward—what new questions did it raise? What new lines of inquiry did it open? What would others want to study based on this research?

In this section, discuss how the study advances future research indicating whether the topic studied warrants additional inquiry and, if so, suggesting the research design for further studies.

Examples

- Alignment of the elementary science curriculum with the current basal reader programs could offer additional insight about how teachers can integrate additional strategy instruction into the science content area. Expanding the two original research questions may lead to continued inquiry into how teachers use reading strategies with expository text in grades 2–5 could offer additional insight into strategies that teachers can implement in their own classrooms. Other research opportunities exist with regard to the cultural aspects of working with populations of students who have high levels of poverty and how the cultural aspect affects their performance in reading. Opportunities for research also exist about integrating the reading strategies across the curriculum of the content areas in order the cross the borders of the content areas using a variety and exposure to many types of expository text. Opportunities for research also exist about integrating the reading strategies across the curriculum of the content areas in order to cross the borders of the content areas using a variety and exposure to many types of expository text. (Fetters, 2010, p. 130)

- Using techniques similar to those utilized in this study it would be possible to perform analyses of other governmental programs to determine if performance-based initiatives were having impact in other areas. . . . Again depending upon the availability of data, programs funding higher education could be analyzed in other states. Finally, additional work could be done . . . to see if other measures not considered in this study were negatively impacted during the duration of the performance-based funding system. Did community programs suffer? Did the quality of graduates entering the state university system decline? Was access to the institutions decreased for at-risk populations that would be less likely to achieve the desired outcomes? (Phillips, 2002, p. 69)

IMPLICATIONS FOR PRACTICE AND RECOMMENDATIONS

The researcher discusses how the study's results contribute to practice, describing the study's influence on practice (Brown, 1997). The discussion, although speculative, presents a rational approach to the impact of the study's results (Skelton and Edwards, 2000) and does not convey an unsubstantiated set of results. In some professional fields, researchers do not speak to practice, instead they recommend specific actions related to policy or other pertinent areas (Baron, 2005).

Examples

- As Polio (2003) points out, there are very few qualitative studies in second language research, and of those, even fewer are naturalistic inquiry. If descriptive studies are instructive rather than prescriptive (Macbeth, 2004) and if, as Gallas (1998) believes, understanding must precede prescription, then it would seem that the field could benefit from more naturalistic inquiry. Second language writing for graduate students who are cultural strangers has been taken up more enthusiastically (e.g., Belcher, 1989; Brandt, 1992; Casanave, 1995; Fox, 1991; Prior, 1995) than interest in "ordinary worlds" of basic, or entry level, cultural strangers. In the literature, there is a marked preference for programs of curricular or instructional engineering. . . . Although these studies are clearly interested in socio-cultural influences, those influences are usually regarded as formal mechanisms in broad macro-cultural (and thus cognitive) terms. A case based program of naturalistic inquiry yielding tutorials for practitioners would proceed in a very different fashion. (Macbeth, 2004, p. 220)
- The implications are directed toward the 4-H professionals in the North Carolina Cooperative Extension Service. The implications may also have utility with the 4-H profession nationally and the North Carolina Cooperative Extension Service Personal and Organization Development system, for validation of the competencies. The following were considered to be the most significant implications. (Burke, 2002, pp. 99–100)
- The most relevant example from this research for developing online communities of museum educators and teachers is the notion of an online community of practice. This could be structured as one section of a larger educational museum web site with several different areas. Allowing participants to choose and easily access the areas of the discussion that are relevant for them is essential. It is important to have a mix of teachers and museum educators as peripheral participants

and as full participants. Additionally, instead of having the policies related to who can post to the community dominated by institutional fear of inappropriate content, it is important to allow the community members access to post information and to allow the community as a group to censure any inappropriate content. (Buffington, 2004, p. 217)

RELATIONSHIP OF RESULTS/FINDINGS TO THEORY

> **Quick Tip:** The researcher is now part of a research tradition. The study adds to the research knowledge base.

The researcher demonstrates the relationship of the results/findings to the theories the researcher used as a foundation for the research. The researcher identifies any emerging theory that contributes to the explanation of the results/findings.

Examples

- The conceptual frameworks for this study were phenomenological theory, social support theory, and health belief model. Fear and anxiety about the disease reflected patterns of phenomenological theory where patients openly shared situations that they had encountered while suffering from chronic hypertensive cardiovascular disease. Consistent with van Manen's (1990) perspective, the patients and caregivers rendered their experiences through story-telling. For example, one patient expressed her fear of becoming too stressed and her fear of having a heart attack or a stroke. . . . A theory as proposed by Harding (1981) states that many African Americans believe that because they have survived the encounter of slavery that they are almost invincible. This health belief termed "fatalism" is one of the reasons why there are African Americans who do not see hypertension as a threat (Vaughan, 1993). "Fatalism" is defined as the belief that since African Americans have been through so much in this country (i.e., slavery, poverty, pain and mental anguish from past experiences) that hypertension is not perceived as a threat. Some evidence of this theory was supported by one patient's comment about her life of trials. (Lang, 2003, p. 94)

- Both the conceptual and theoretical frameworks of this study identify the quantifiable background characteristics, precollege experiences and specific in-college experiences that can theoretically impact students' ASR. Whereas human capital theory posits that the development of ASR—such as volunteerism, community service, or civic engagement—are highly valued within society because of the substantial public or external benefits they provide; social capital theory suggests that altruism can be a cause and an outcome, where one's network of connections to relationships and norms and an individual's social environment can promote the development of altruism and social responsibility, yet altruistic and social responsible behavior can also be a means to generate more social capital; and cultural capital theory explains that cultural resources and knowledge, including altruism and social responsibility, are transferred across generations in home, school, college, and other social environments, as a means of maintaining or advancing social status. Together, human, social, and cultural capital guide our understanding of students' own characteristics and perceptions, as well as the effects and outcomes of their involvement in and engagement with specific aspects of their college experiences. College impact research aims to identify and statistically control for the effects of precollege factors in order to better isolate and estimate the impact of curriculum, co-curriculum, and other specific college experiences on a given student outcome such as ASR, the outcome of focus in the present study. (Padgett, 2011, p. 112)

LIMITATIONS

Quick Tip: Identify limitations that emerged during the study but were unknown at the onset of the study.

In this section, the researcher discusses the limitations of the study related to validity, reliability, credibility, trustworthiness, and other methodological issues that were unforeseen and became apparent during the conduct of the study. The discussion of the study's newly identified limitations links the study's limitations to potential future studies modeling this research (Heath, 1997).

Examples

- A number of limitations require attention when interpreting the results of the current study. First, due to time constraints and lower then predicted numbers of individuals attending follow-up appointments, this study had a smaller sample size than was initially desired. Additionally, some participants failed to complete all questionnaires administered, typically due to an error such as missing a full page of items before returning their forms by mail. Thus, in order to maximize N in each analysis, data were used for all participants who completed at least some of the administered instruments at all time points. Therefore, sample size was variable across analyses, leading to slight variations in the participants included in separate analyses. (Keedy, 2009, p. 104)

- There were several limitations to this study that restrict the generalization of its results. The results of the present study have been generated by the validation procedure outlined in Chapter 3 during four successive semesters (Fall 1999 to Spring 2001) at the Pennsylvania State University and Arizona State University. The sample consisted of sophomore to graduate level students enrolled in modern physics, undergraduate quantum mechanics, graduate quantum mechanics, and graduate chemistry quantum mechanics courses. The sample size was 146 students in all groups combined. Ideally, more students should be involved in a validation study (Nunnally, 1978). Due to the nature of the concepts and the unique population, it would have been extremely difficult to administer several iterations to hundreds of students as recommended by some experts. Due to the small sample size and due to the limited number of universities involved in the study, however, caution is warranted in interpreting results, especially in Chapter 4 section 4.5 a–e. While the students who have participated in this study were most likely representative of groups in similar universities, caution is warranted in applying these findings to other populations since, for example, the students were predominantly male. . . . Data gathered in this validation study were gathered principally from volunteers whose final course grades were not based upon their performance on the QMVI. (Cataloglu, 2002, pp. 117–18)

SUMMARY AND CONCLUSION

The summary and conclusion are comprehensive summative statements of the researcher's study. In this section the researcher highlights the important aspects of the study, suggests future research,
and provides a strong closing statement.

Examples

- Social movements have become an increasingly prevalent aspect of American society (Macionis, 1995). Organizations have
  distinguished themselves both by their willingness to respond
  to these movements and their reluctance to do so. This wide
  range of responses raises the question, under what conditions
  do firms respond to social movements? The results of this
  study suggest that public support and industry attention to
  the movement facilitate organizational action. Contrary to expectations, direct governmental coercion had little influence
  over organizations. These results offer several implications for
  theoretical development. First, they suggest that contrary to
  conventional assumptions institutional environments are not
  monolithic in terms of their influence over firms. Different
  institutional forces appear to exert different pressures on
  firms. This suggests that institutional environments may be
  more complex than previously expected. Second, the results
  failed to support the notion that the government can force
  action. This suggests that the real power to facilitate organizational action and social change may lie in public acceptance
  and visibility of social concerns. These findings provide the
  basis for future examinations and explanations of this complex phenomenon. (Bergh, 2002, pp. 64–65)
- In conclusion, this study was an attempt to investigate the
  dynamic socialization process using a more comprehensive
  cognition, affect, behavior framework and by testing longitudinal, mediated relationships. Unidirectional causation and
  person-situation interactions are important, especially for theory development, however research must become more comprehensive as theory becomes more developed. This study
  has shown that stable individual differences, cognition, affect,
  and behavior (information seeking and performance behavior) are important in newcomer socialization. They are inter-
  dependent and should not necessarily be thought of as out-

comes. This study has also shown that socialization patterns appear to generalize to blue-collar workers and part time workers. Although this study failed to provide compelling evidence in support of cyclical recursive relationships, these type of relationships are important, seem highly probable, and require more attention in future research. (Brink, 2003, p. 104)

Pep Talk

Celebrate! The goal is achieved. Rest, relax, recoup. A new adventure awaits. The researcher uses what was learned through the process to help build a better, more sustainable world.

> I have been impressed with the urgency of doing. Knowing is not enough; we must apply. Being willing is not enough, we must do.
> —Leonardo da Vinci

Appendix

Advice on References, Plagiarism, Quoting, Paraphrasing, and Summarizing

REFERENCES

In the reference list, the researcher includes every cited reference. The researcher does not include references not cited in the text (Bartness, 1999). Department norms determine the citation style for the researcher's references. Frequently used stylistic systems are APA (American Psychological Association), MLA (Modern Language Association), and CMS (Chicago Manual of Style).

PLAGIARISM

Plagiarism is intellectual theft. "It is using another person's words or ideas without giving credit to the other person. . . . [Y]ou must put quotation marks around them and give the writer or speaker credit by revealing the source in a citation" (Harris, 2004, para. 5). Researchers make a good faith commitment to give credit to all sources in writing their dissertations. Stress associated with writing the dissertation may tempt a researcher to take intellectual short-cuts, including cutting and pasting another's work. These actions threaten the foundation of academia and erode future credibility. In academia, researchers trust one another as the basis for the pursuit of new knowledge. They share ideas, work, and credit.

Avoiding plagiarism is easy, provided the researcher gives credit where credit is due. Some excellent database software programs make it easy to provide citations. In the following quote, I provide the citation for the quote with the Endnote software program. Since I wrote this book in APA style, quotes more than forty words are blocked without using quotation marks, as follows:

You cite your sources to give credit to those people whose ideas/ words you are using in your paper and to distinguish their ideas/ words from your own ideas and words; to make your argument stronger. Doing research on an issue strengthens your position, because it shows you have engaged with some of the other positions on your topic and incorporated them into your thinking; to allow your readers to verify your claims and to get more information from the source materials. (Emory University Libraries, 2004, para. 1)

QUOTING, PARAPHRASING, AND SUMMARIZING

The researcher, when quoting, ensures the quote is accurate. The researcher uses quotation marks or another appropriate format (depending on the department norms for the style guide) indicating the material is a quote.

Use direct quotations only when the author's wording is necessary or particularly effective. If you are using material cited by an author and you do not have the original source, introduce the quotation with a phrase such as "as quoted in . . ." Place all direct quotations within quotation marks, or indent them if using block quotes. Be sure to copy quotations exactly as they appear. (Revere, 2004)

The researcher, when paraphrasing, adapts the source material into the researcher's words and sentence structure conveying the author's ideas and meaning (Morgan, 2004; Indiana University, 2004). A summary is generally shorter than paraphrasing, but the source of the summary must also be cited (Purdue University, 2001). The bottom line for researchers is this: When in doubt, cite.

References

Abercrombie-Donahue, M. (2011). *Educators' perceptions of Indian education for all: A tribal critical race theory ethnography.* (EdD), Montana State University, Bozeman, MT.

Ackerman, J. (2003). *Delinquents and their friends: The role of peer effects and self-selection.* (PhD), The Pennsylvania State University.

Adams, E. H. (2002). *Community-based programming: Perceived levels of utility, practice, and encouragement among North Carolina Community College mid-level managers.* (EdD), North Carolina State University, Raleigh, NC. Retrieved from http://www.lib.ncsu.edu/theses/available/etd-04262002-130540/unrestricted/etd.pdf.

Adams, G. (2004). *Power plays: A longitudinal examination of CEO/BOD power circulation and its impact on organizational performance.* (PhD), Florida State University, Tallahassee, FL. Retrieved from http://etd.lib.fsu.edu/theses/available/etd-07092004-161044/unrestricted/Dissertation_Final.pdf.

Afolabi, M. (1992). The review of related literature. *International Journal of Information and Library, 4*(1), 59—66.

Agency for Healthcare Research and Qualtiy. (2005). *Essentials of the research plan.* Agency for Healthcare Research and Quality. Rockville, MD. Retrieved from http://www.ahrq.gov/fund/esstplan.htm.

Akbulut, A. (2003). *An investigation of the factors that influence electronic information sharing between state and local agencies.* (PhD), Louisiana State University, Baton Rouge, LA. Retrieved from http://etd02.lnx390.lsu.edu/docs/available/etd-0619103-214616/unrestricted/05CHAPTER4.pdf.

Alexander, A. (2004). *A qualitative exploration of students' experiences with tutorial learning.* (PhD), Louisiana State University and Agricultural and Mechanical College, Baton Rouge, LA.

Allgood, J. (2003). *Initiation of treatment for alcohol abuse: A developmental approach.* (PhD), Florida State University. Retrieved from http://etd.lib.fsu.edu/theses/available/etd-09182003-211751/unrestricted/allgooddissertation.pdf.

Alzate, M. (2002). *The quality of life of single mothers on welfare in Georgia and the 1996 welfare reform.* (PhD), University of Georgia, Athens, GA. Retrieved from http://dbs.galib.uga.edu/cgi-bin/ultimate.cgi?dbs=getd&userid=galileo&action=search&_cc=1

American Psychological Association. (2010). *Publication manual of the American Psychological Association* (5th ed.). Washington, D.C.: American Psychological Association.

Ammon, S. C. (2002). *Global economics, domestic politics, and reforms of social Insurance programs in advanced capitalist countries.* (PhD), The University of Tennessee, Knoxville, TN. Retrieved from http://etd.library.vanderbilt.edu/ETD-db/theses/available/etd-0329102-130816/unrestricted/etd.pdf.

Anderson, A. (2003). *A descriptive study of the criteria used for school choice selection and preference among African American parents/caregivers in an integrated magnet school district of choice.* (EdD), Seton Hall University, South Orange, NJ.

Anderson, A. (2009). *Assumptions constructing a school superintendent's mental model for technology use.* (EdD), Montana State University, Bozeman, MT.

Andre, P., Bitondo, D., Berthelot, M., and Louillet, D. (2001). Development of conceptual and methodological frameworks for the integrated assessment of the impacts of linear infrastructure projects on quality of life. Retrieved on February 17, 2005, from http://www.ceaa-acee.gc.ca/015/0002/0015/5_e.htm.

Babbie, E. (2001). *The practice of social research* (9th ed.). Belmont, CA: Wadsworth.

Baehr, A. (2004). *Wounded healers and relational experts: A grounded theory of experienced psychotherapists' management and use of counter transference.* (PhD), The Pennsylvania State University, University Park, PA. Retrieved from http://etda.libraries.psu.edu/theses/approved/WorldWideFiles/ETD-565/baehr.pdf.

Bailey, K. (2002). *The effects of learning strategies on student interaction and student satisfaction.* (PhD), The Pennsylvania State University, University Park, PA. Retrieved from http://etda.libraries.psu.edu/theses/approved/WorldWideFiles/ETD-130/Thesis.pdf.

Baron, M. (2005). Guidelines for writing research proposals and dissertations. Retrieved May 10, 2012, from http://people.usd.edu/~mbaron/edad885/Dissertation Guide.pdf.

Bartness, T. (1999). Department of Psychology dissertation guidelines. Retrieved on May 12, 2005, from http://www.gsu.edu/psychology/PsycDeptDissertationGuidelines.doc.

Becker, K. (2007). *Unlearning in the workplace: A mixed methods study.* (PhD), Queensland University of Technology, Queensland AU.

Bedell, T. (2002). *The role of religiosity in forgiveness.* (PhD), The Ohio State University, Columbus, OH. Retrieved from http://www.ohiolink.edu/etd/send-pdf.cgi?osu1039114801.

Beloney-Morrison, T. (2003). *Your blues ain't like mine: Exploring the promotion and tenure process of African American female professors at select research I universities in the South.* (PhD), Louisiana State University, Baton Rouge, LA. Retrieved from http://etd02.lnx390.lsu.edu/docs/submitted/etd-1107103-100118/unrestricted/Beloney.pdf.

Bergh, J. (2002). *Do social movements matter to organizations? An institutional theory perspective on corporate responses to the contemporary environmental movement.* (PhD), The Pennsylvania State University, University Park, PA. Retrieved from http://etda.libraries.psu.edu/theses/approved/WorldWideFiles/ETD-191/bergh.etd.pdf.

Berkowitz, S. (1997). Chapter 4: Analyzing qualitative data. Retrieved from http://www.ehr.nsf.gov/EHR/REC/pubs/NSF97-153/CHAP_4.HTM.

Blankenship, K. (2004). *Looking for success: Transition planning for students with visual impairments in the State of Iowa.* (PhD), Vanderbilt University, Nashville, TN. Retrieved from http://etd.library.vanderbilt.edu/ETD-db/available/etd-11302004-105924/unrestricted/etd.pdf.

Bodur, Y. (2003). *Preservice teachers' learning of multiculturalism in a teacher education program.* (PhD), Florida State University, Tallahassee, FL. Retrieved from http://etd.lib.fsu.edu/theses/available/etd-11152003-001519/unrestricted/02_YB_text_pdf.pdf.

Bond, C. (2004). *Does increasing Black homeownership decrease residential segregation?* (PhD), University of Notre Dame, South Bend, IN. Retrieved from http://etd.nd.edu/ETD-db/theses/available/etd-04102004-102114/unrestricted/BondCB042004.pdf.

Bondima, M. H. (2004). The nature of culturally responsive pedagogy in two urban African American middle school science classrooms. Unpublished PhD, University of Maryland College Park, College Park, MD.

Bradley, L., Flathouse, P., Gould, L., Hendricks, C., and Robinson, B. (1994, November 5, 1994). The basics of dissertation writing, 2004, from http://www.bamaed.ua.edu/~kcarmich/WRITING.KDC.htm.

Brink, K. (2003). *New hire socialization: The dynamic relationships among individual differences, cognition, affect, and behavior.* (PhD), University of Georgia, Athens, GA. Retrieved from http://dbs.galib.uga.edu/cgi-bin/ultimate.cgi?dbs=getd&userid=galileo&action=search&_cc=1.

Brown, H. (1997). Writing your dissertation, 2004, from http://www.educ.hku.hk/student/manual/dissert2.htm - step3.

Buffington, M. (2004). Using the Internet to develop students' critical thinking skills and build online communities of teachers: A review of research with implications for museum education. Unpublished PhD, Ohio State University, Columbus, OH.

Bumkrant, S. (2003). Interrater agreement of incumbent job specification importance ratings: Rater, occupation, and item effects. Blacksburg, VA: Virginia Polytechnic Institute and State University.

Burke, T. (2002). *Defining competency and reviewing factors that may impact knowledge perceived importance and use of competence in the 4-H professional's job.* (PhD), North Carolina State University, Raleigh, NC. Retrieved from http://www.lib.ncsu.edu/theses/available/etd-11222002-101125/unrestricted/etd.pdf.

Burnard, P. (2004). Writing a qualitative research report. *Accident and Emergency Nursing, 12,* 176–81.

Cain, S. (2003). *A comparison of community members preference to viewing two different approaches to therapy.* (PhD), West Virginia University, Morgantown, WV. Retrieved from http://kitkat.wvu.edu:8080/files/2945.1.cain_sherry_dissertation.pdf.

Calabrese, R., Sheppard, D., Hummel, C., Laramore, C., and Nance, E. (2005). Identifying teachers' and administrators' perceptions of the efficacy of the impact of professional development on the quality of teacher instruction. Wichita, KS: Wichita State University.

Calabrese, R., Sherwood, K., Fast, J., and Womack, C. (2003). Pay for performance plans in selected school districts: A systematic literature review. Wichita, KS: Wichita State University.

Capacci-Carneal, C. (2004). *Community schools in Mali: A multilevel analysis.* (PhD), Florida State University, Tallahassee, FL. Retrieved from http://etd.lib.fsu.edu/theses/available/etd-07122004-143940/unrestricted/01_ccc_dissertation.pdf.pdf.

Carper, A. (2002). *Bright students in a wasteland: The at-risk gifted, a qualitative study of fourteen gifted dropouts.* (EdD), North Carolina State University, Raleigh, NC. Retrieved from http://www.lib.ncsu.edu/theses/available/etd-10082002-154536/unrestricted/etd.pdf.

Carpiniello, K. (2004). The development of adolescent panic, depression, and alcohol expectancies as a function of anxiety sensitivity. Unpublished PhD, Fordham University, New York, NY.

Carraway, J. (2112). *Principals' sensemaking of the implementation of skillful observation and coaching laboratory.* (EdD), North Carolina State University, Raleigh, NC.

Cataloglu, E. (2002). *Development and validation of an achievement test in introductory quantum mechanics: The quantum mechanics visualization instrument*

(QMVI). (PhD), The Pennsylvania State University, University Park, PA. Retrieved from http://etda.libraries.psu.edu/theses/approved/WorldWideFiles/ETD-145/thesis.pdf.

Chae, M. (2006). *The development of a conceptual framework for identifying functional, expressive, aesthetic, and regulatory needs for snowboarding helmets*. (PhD), Virginia Polytechnic Institute and State University, Blacksburg, VA.

Chappelear, T. C. (2011). *The relationship of teachers' perceptions of high school principal's monitoring student progress and student achievement in southeastern Ohio*. (EdD), West Virginia University.

Chein, J. (2004). *Evaluating models of working memory: FMRI and behavioral evidence on the effects of concurrent irrelevant information*. (PhD), The University of Pittsburgh, Pittsburgh, PA. Retrieved from http://etd.library.pitt.edu/ETD/available/etd-03262004-162700/unrestricted/Chein_5-04_Dissertation.pdf.

Childs, M. (2010). *Learners' experience of presence in virtual worlds*. (PhD), University of Warick, Institute, Warwick, UK.

Clark, D., Guba, E., and Smith, G. (1977). *Functions and definitions of functions of a research proposal*. Indiana University. Bloomington, IN. Retrieved from http://polaris.gseis.ucla.edu/jrichardson/dis290/clark.pdf

Cobb, C. (2010). *Minoritized parents, special education, and inclusion*. (PhD), University of Toronto, Toronto, CA.

Cochran, G. (2009). *Ohio State University Extension competency study: Developing a competency model for a 21st century extension organization*. (PhD), The Ohio State University, Columbus, OH.

Collins, J. (2004). *Adult and community college education*. (PhD), North Carolina State University, Raleigh, NC. Retrieved from http://www.lib.ncsu.edu/theses/available/etd-05102004-010437/unrestricted/etd.pdf.

Colorado State University School of Education. (2001). Dissertation guide, 2004, from http://soegrad.colostate.edu/pubs/DissertationGuide.pdf.

Columbia University School of Nursing. (2003). *Doctor of nursing science program student handbook*. New York, NY: Columbia University.

Cooper, E. (2002). *Living in the question: An inward journey to the heart of the practice of inquiry*. (EdD), University of Cincinnati, Cincinnati, OH. Retrieved from http://www.ohiolink.edu/etd/send-pdf.cgi?acc_num=ucin1029337057.

Crotogino, J. (2002). Visual stress in migraine: Subjective and psychophysiological responses to intense visual stimulation. Unpublished PhD, McGill University, Montreal, Canada.

Cupples, C. (2010). *Characterizing dietary intake and physical activity affecting weight gain in kidney transplant recipients*. (PhD), The University of Tennessee Health Science Center, Knoxville, TN.

D'Angelo, P. (2002). CA 5000 Communication Research: Proposal Assignments, from http://www16.homepage.villanova.edu/paul.dangelo/comm5000/Proposal Assignments.htm.

Dejoy, S. (2011). *The role of male partners in childbirth decision making: A qualitative exploration with first-time parenting couples*. (PhD), University of South Florida, Tampa, FL.

Denton, E. (2011). *Elementary principals' strategies for managing the educational technology refresh process: A case study*. (EdD), Temple University, Philadelphia, PA.

DeWitz, S. J. (2004). *Exploring the relationship between self-efficacy beliefs and purpose in life*. (PhD), The Ohio State University, Columbus, OH. Retrieved from http://www.ohiolink.edu/etd/send-pdf.cgi?osu1087834931.

Drotos, S. (2011). *"Secret ingredients" in postsecondary educational attainment: Challenges faced by students attending high poverty high schools*. (PhD), The Ohio

State University, Columbus, OH. Retrieved from http://etd.ohiolink.edu/view.cgi?acc_num=osu1299170270.

Duncanson, E. (2003). *The impact of classroom organization in grade 4 on student achievement in science.* (EdD), Seton Hall, South Orange, NJ. Retrieved from http://domapp01.shu.edu/depts/uc/apps/libraryrepository.nsf/resourceid/94D6A737145C25F585256E1A006CF12E/$File/Duncanson-Edward_Doctorate.pdf?Open.

Edwards, B. (2007). *Studies in tobacco harm reduction: The role of context in subjective effects and behavioral responses to a reduced exposure tobacco product.* (PhD), The Pennsylvania State University, University Park, PA.

El-Ashry, F. (2009). *General education pre-service teachers' attitudes toward inclusion in Egypt.* (PhD), University of Florida, Gainesville, FL.

Emory University Libraries. (2004). Citing your sources and plagiarism, part 4, Citation styles and citing sources. Retrieved on April 24, 2005, from http://web.library.emory.edu/services/ressvcs/citation/plagiarismpart4.html#why cite.

Engle, M. (2003). In distinguishing scholarly journals from other periodicals, from http://www.library.cornell.edu/olinuris/ref/research/skill20.html.

Eteokleous, N. (2004). *Computer technology integration in Cyprus elementary schools.* (PhD), The Pennsylvania State University. Retrieved from http://etda.libraries.psu.edu/theses/approved/WorldWideFiles/ETD-677/dissertation_final_new1.pdf.

Farrell, A. (2006). *Why women don't watch women's sport: A qualitative analysis.* (PhD), The Ohio State University, Columbus, OH.

Fast, J. (2005). *A study of the aspirations of the Goessel Unified School District, USD 411.* (EdD), Wichita State University, Wichita, KS.

Feldman, D. (2003). What Are We Talking About When We Talk About Theory? *Journal of Management, 30*(5).

Fetters, C. (2010). *An exploration of strategy-based reading instruction using expository science text in grades 2–5.* (PhD), Louisiana State University and Agricultural and Mechanical College, Baton Rouge, LA.

Franco, W. (2003). Hydrodynamics and control in thermal-fluid networks. Unpublished PhD, University of Notre Dame, South Bend, IN.

Fretz, K. (2006). *Engineering-based probabilistic risk assessment for food safety with application to Escherichia Coli 0157:H7 contamination in cheese.* (PhD), University of Maryland, College Park, MD.

Gade, C. J. (2003). *An exploration of the pharmacist-patient communicative relationship.* (PhD), The Ohio State University, Columbus, OH. Retrieved from http://www.ohiolink.edu/etd/send-pdf.cgi?osu1061259087.

Gage, C. Q. (2003). *The meaning and measure of school mindfulness: An exploratory analysis.* (PhD), The Ohio State University, Columbus, OH. Retrieved from http://www.ohiolink.edu/etd/view.cgi?acc_num=osu1069683954.

Gaines, J. (2001). *Worry and associated symptoms in younger versus middle-aged adults with DSM-IV Generalized Anxiety Disorder at pre- and post-treatment.* (PhD), The Pennsylvania State University, University Park, PA. Retrieved from http://etda.libraries.psu.edu/theses/approved/WorldWideFiles/ETD-101/jeffgainesETD.pdf.

Geise, M. (2011). *A longitudinal analysis of outcomes associated with Ohio's postsecondary enrollment options program.* (PhD), Bowling Green State University, Bowling Green, OH.

Georgia Institute of Technology School of Civil and Environmental Engineering. (2001). Scientific approaches for transportation research, 2005, from http://traffic.ce.gatech.edu/nchrp2045/v1chapter5.html.

Gerlach, J. (2009). *An examination of factors that explain the use of data in the natural resource policy process*. (PhD), North Carolina State University, Raleigh, NC.

Glatthorn, A. (1998). *Writing the winning dissertation*. Thousand Oaks, CA: Corwin Press.

Godfrey, P. (2003). *Listening to students' and teachers' voices: An ecological case study investigating the transition from elementary to middle school*. (PhD), North Carolina State University, Raleigh, NC. Retrieved from http://www.lib.ncsu.edu/theses/available/etd-04092003-142316/unrestricted/etd .pdf.

Gohn, J. (2004). *Signs of change: The role of team leadership and culture in science education reform*. (PhD), Miami University, Oxford, OH. Retrieved from http://www.ohiolink.edu/etd/send-pdf.cgi?acc_num=miami1083173492.

Gossett, J. (2002). *Economic development and community colleges: Attributes, attitudes and satisfaction levels of western North Carolina stakeholders*. (EdD), North Carolina State University, Raleigh, NC. Retrieved from http://www.lib.ncsu.edu/theses/available/etd-10242002-172928/unrestricted/etd .pdf.

Gradwell, S. (2004). Communicating planned change: A case study of leadership credibility. Unpublished PhD, Drexel University, Philadelphia, PA.

Greenberg, A. L. (2011). *Addressing the research-to-practice gap in autism treatments: Applying an effectiveness research model to the picture exchange communication system*. (PhD), The Claremont Graduate University, Claremont, CA. ProQuest Dissertations and Theses, retreived from http://search.proquest.com/docview/863687258?accountid=9783.

Guba, E., and Lincoln, Y. (1981). *Effective evaluation: Improving the usefulness of evaluation results through responsive and naturalistic approaches*. San Francisco, CA: Jossey-Bass.

Hall, H. (2008). *The relationships among adaptive behaviors of children with autism spectrum disorder, their family support networks, parental stress, and parental coping*. (PhD), The University of Tennessee, Knoxville, TN.

Hanson, M. A. (2004). *Predicting the distribution of a goodness-of-fit statistic appropriate for use with performance-based assessments*. (PhD), University of Pittsburgh, Pittsburgh, PA. Retrieved from http://etd.library.pitt.edu/ETD/available/etd-12112004-230948/unrestricted/HansenMaryADissertation1204.pdf.

Harris, R. (2004). Anti-plagiarism strategies for research papers. Retrieved on May 3, 2005, from http://www.virtualsalt.com/antiplag.htm.

Heath, A. (1997). The proposal in qualitative research. *Qualitative Report*, 3(1).

Heffner, C. (2004a). Research Methods. Retrieved on April 19, 2005, from http://allpsych.com/researchmethods/index.html.

Heffner, C. (2004b). Test validity and reliability. Retrieved on December 4, 2004, from http://allpsych.com/researchmethods/validityreliability.html.

Hinds, D. (2008). *Social network structure as a critical success in condition for open source software project communities*. (PhD), Florida International University, Miami, FL.

Hoare, I. (2007). *Attitudinal factors related to driving behaviors of young adults in Belize: An application of the precaution adoption process model*. (PhD), University of South Florida, Tampa, FL.

Hoffman, K. (2003). *The "dark side" of self esteem: Examining the relation between overly-positive self-perceptions and aggressive behavior in adolescents*. (PhD), University of Notre Dame, South Bend, IN. Retrieved from http://etd.nd.edu/ETD-db/theses/available/etd-12042003-114249/unrestricted/HoffmanK122 003.pdf.

Horak, J. J. (2002). *Factors predicting distress at marital therapy onset.* (PhD), Western Michigan University, Kalamazoo, MI. ProQuest Dissertations and Theses, retreived from http://search.proquest.com/docview/275967635?accountid=9783.

House, C. (2004). *Out and about: Predictors of lesbians' outness in the workplace.* (PhD), The Pennsylvania State University, University Park, PA. Retrieved from http://etda.libraries.psu.edu/theses/approved/WorldWideFiles/ETD-512/etd.pdf.

Hughes, C. (2008). Performance for learning: How emotions play a part. (PhD), The Ohio State University, Columbus, OH.

Hutchinson, J. (2004). *Psychological factors in perceived and sustained effort.* (PhD), Florida State University, Tallahassee, FL. Retrieved from http://etd.lib.fsu.edu/theses/available/etd-07092004-135618/unrestricted/jasmin_hutchinson_dissertation.pdf.

Indiana University. (2004). Plagiarism: What it is and how to recognize and avoid it. Instructional Support Services, Writing Tutorial Services. Retrieved on May 6, 2005, from http://www.indiana.edu/~wts/pamphlets/plagiarism.shtml.

International University of Professional Studies. (2004, January, 25, 2004). Dissertation manual, from http://64.233.167.104/search?q=cache:9vfRM8oFZGwJ:www.iups.edu/IUPS_Dissertation_Manual_rev_2-1-04.pdf+%22chapter+one%22+%22dissertation+help%22&hl=en.

Johnson, D. K. (2002). *General education 2000—a national survey: How general education changed between 1989 and 2000.* (PhD), The Pennsylvania State University, University Park, PA. Retrieved from http://etda.libraries.psu.edu/theses/approved/WorldWideFiles/ETD-201/thesis.pdf.

Johnson, D. M. (2002). *The role of initial coping strategies on subsequent appointment attendance in individuals with HIV: A longitudinal analysis.* (PhD), Louisiana State University, Baton Rouge, LA. Retrieved from http://etd02.lnx390.lsu.edu/docs/available/etd-0417102-092007/unrestricted/07methods.pdf.

Joppe, M. (2004). The research process, 2004, from http://www.ryerson.ca/%7Emjoppe/rp.htm.

Karchmer, M. (1996). An alternative dissertation research model, from http://gradschool.gallaudet.edu/dissertation/appendixl.html.

Karchmer, M., and Johnson, R. (1996). Dissertation handbook, from http://gradschool.gallaudet.edu/dissertation/overview.html.

Keedy, N. (2009). *Health locus of control, self-efficacy, and multidisciplinary intervention for chronic back pain.* (PhD), University of Iowa, Iowa City, IA.

Keeler, C. (2003). *Developing and using an instrument to describe instructional design elements of high school online courses.* (PhD), University of Oregon, Eugene, OR. Retrieved from http://www.pdkintl.org/edres/ddwin_ra.pdf.

Kennedy, I. (2004). How to do research, from http://www.geocities.com/Athens/3238/page3-15.htm.

Kitchenham, B. (2004). Procedures for performing systematic reviews. Eversleigh, AU: Keele University Technical Report.

Koh, K. (2011). *Proposing a theoretical framework for digital age youth information behavior bulding upon radical change theory.* (PhD), Florida State University, Tallahassee, FL.

Krabacher, A. (2008). *Undergraduate research as a means of student engagement: A study of research's involvement in five areas of college life.* (PhD), The Ohio State University, Columbus, OH.

Krumme, G. (2000). Phases, stages, and steps in geographic investigation and research. Retrieved December 6, 2005, from http://faculty.washington.edu/~krumme/guides/researchguide.html - frame.

Krumme, G. (2002). Economic geography: Toward a conceptual framework, from http://faculty.washington.edu/~krumme/gloss/c.html – concept.

Kyzer, M. (2001). *Empathy, creativity, and conflict resolution in adolescents.* (PhD), University of Georgia, Athens, GA. Retrieved from http://dbs.galib.uga.edu/cgi-bin/ultimate.cgi?dbs=getd&userid=galileo&action=search&_cc=1.

Lang, L. (2003). Expressed coping strategies and techniques among African American families in north Florida who are living with chronic hypertensive cardiovascular disease. Unpublished PhD, Florida State University, Tallahassee, FL.

LeJeune, E. (2001). Critical analysis, from http://www.selu.edu/Academics/Faculty/elejeune/critique.htm.

Long, J. F. (2003). *Connecting with the content: How teacher interest affects student interest in a core course.* (PhD), The Ohio State University, Columbus, OH. Retrieved from http://www.ohiolink.edu/etd/send-pdf.cgi?acc_num=osu1056140146.

Luseno, F. K. (2001). *An assessment of the perceptions of secondary special and general education teachers working in inclusive settings in the Commonwealth of Virginia.* (PhD), Virginia Polytechnic Institute and State University, Blacksburg, VA. Retrieved from http://scholar.lib.vt.edu/theses/available/etd-02132001-003827/unrestricted/FlosElectronicDissertation.pdf.

Macbeth, K. (2004). *The situated achievements of novices learning academic writing as a cultural curriculum.* (PhD), The Ohio State University, Columbus, OH. Retrieved from http://www.ohiolink.edu/etd/send-pdf.cgi?osu1101244159.

Mather, M. (2004). *The contextual, academic, and socio-cultural factors influencing kindergarten students' mathematical literacy development.* (PhD), University of Toledo, Toledo, OH. Retrieved from http://www.ohiolink.edu/etd/send-pdf.cgi?toledo1102883081.

Mattingly, M. (2003). A study of superintendents' practices of principal supervision and evaluation: A contrast of low performing and performing schools. Unpublished EdD, University of Georgia, Athens, GA.

McCord, P. (2010). *The influence of teacher characteristics on preference for models of teaching.* (EdD), University of Southern California, Los Angelus, CA.

McCutcheon, A. (2010). *Impact of publishers' policy on electronic thesis and dissertation (ETD) distribution options within the United States.* (PhD), Ohio University, Athens, OH.

Merriam, S. (2001). *Qualitative research and case study applications in education* (2nd ed.). San Francisco, CA: Jossey-Bass Publishers.

Merriam, S. (2002). *Qualitative research in practice: Examples for discussion and analysis.* San Francisco, CA: Jossey-Bass Publishers.

Meyer, D. (2003). *Technology's relationship to issues connected to retention: A focus on rural mental health practitioners.* (PhD), Ohio University, Athens, OH. Retrieved from http://www.ohiolink.edu/etd/view.cgi?ohiou1082491212.

Miles, M., and Huberman, A. (1994). *Qualitative data analysis: An expanded sourcebook* (2nd ed.). Thousand Oaks, CA: Sage Publications Inc.

Miller, C. (2004). *A case study of teacher hiring practices in award winning middle schools in Pennsylvania.* (EdD), University of Pittsburgh, Pittsburgh. Retrieved from http://etd.library.pitt.edu/ETD/available/etd-12082004-145133/unrestricted/001millercl09-04.pdf.

Miller, D. (2011). *The power of appreciative inquiry: Discovering the latent potential of an urban high school.* (PhD), The Ohio State University, Columbus, OH.

Miller, L. (2003). *Qualitative investigation of intercollegiate coaches' perceptions of altruistic leadership*. (PhD), The Ohio State University, Columbus, OH. Retrieved from http://www.ohiolink.edu/etd/send-pdf.cgi?acc_num=osu1060 273538.

Morgan, S. (2004). Advice to students: How to avoid plagiarism. Retrieved on May 6, 2006, from http://www.services.unimelb.edu.au/plagiarism/advice.html#avoiding.

Murillo, J. (2005). Murillo method: A guide. Retrieved May 11, 2012, from http://coe.csusb.edu/Murillo/method3.htm.

National Health and Medical Research Council. (2000). *How to review the evidence: Systematic identification and review of the scientific literature*. (1864960329). Canberra, Australia: National Health and Medical Research Council. Retrieved from http://www.nhmrc.gov.au/publications/pdf/cp65.pdf.

Neill, S. (2003). *The identification of effective strategies for bond campaigns in Kansas school districts: An analysis of the beliefs of superintendents who conducted bond issue campaigns*. (EdD), Wichita State University, Wichita, KS.

Neuendorf, K. (2001). The content analysis guidebook online April 15, 2005. Retrieved from http://academic.csuohio.edu/kneuendorf/content/.

Nicolas, M. G. (2002). *A cross-cultural examination of individual values, worry, and mental health status*. (PhD), The Pennsylvania State University, University Park, PA. Retrieved from http://etda.libraries.psu.edu/theses/approved/WorldWideFiles/ETD-123/thesis.pdf.

Nolan, D. (2009). *A study of the relationship of teachers' self-efficacy and the impact of professional learning community as an organizaitonal structure*. (PhD), Louisiana State University and Agricultural and Mechanical College, Baton Rouge, LA.

Olson, J. (2004). *How do preservice teachers learn from early field experiences? Narratives from a cohort in an elementary teacher education program*. (PhD), University of Georgia, Athens, GA. Retrieved from http://dbs.galib.uga.edu/cgi-bin/ultimate.cgi?dbs=getd&userid=galileo&action=search&_cc=1.

Ormondroyd, J. (2003). Critically analyzing information sources, 2004, from http://www.library.cornell.edu/olinuris/ref/research/skill26.htm.

Ormondroyd, J., Engle, M., and Cosgrave, T. (2004). Critically analyzing information sources, 2005, from http://www.library.cornell.edu/olinuris/ref/research/skill26.htm.

Padgett, R. (2011). *The effects of the first year of college on undergraduates' development of altruistic and socially responsible behavior*. (PhD), University of Iowa, Iowa City, IA.

Palmiero, J. (2011). *A study of school board members' views on affiliations with private charitable foundations supporting public education: A regional study situated in Pennsylvania's Allegheny county*. (EdD), University of Pittsburgh, Pittsburgh, PA.

Pane, D. (2009). *The relationship between classroom interactions and exclusionary discipline as a social practice: A critical microethnography*. (PhD), Florida International University, Miami, FL.

Paparone, C. (2003). *Applying the competing values framework to study organizational subcultures and system-wide planning efforts in a military university*. (Phd), The Pennsylvania State University, University Park, PA. Retrieved from http://etda.libraries.psu.edu/theses/approved/WorldWideFiles/ETD-316/PararoneThesis.pdf.

Patton, M. (2002). *Qualitative research and evaluation methods* (3rd ed.). Thousand Oaks: Sage.

Pfaffman, J. (2003). *Manipulating and measuring student engagement in computer-based instruction*. (PhD), Vanderbilt University, Nashville, TN. Retrieved from http://etd.library.vanderbilt.edu/ETD-db/available/etd-11262003-090736/unrestricted/pfaffman.pdf.

Phillips, M. (2002). *The effectiveness of performance-based outcomes in a community college system.* (EdD), University of Florida, Tallahassee, FL.

Pidwirny, M. (2004). Chapter 3: The science of physical geography—Hypothesis testing. Retrieved on May 3, 2005, from http://www.physicalgeography.net/fundamentals/3f.html.

Pierce, L. L. (2009). Twelve steps for success in the nursing research journey. *Journal of Continuing Education in Nursing, 40*(4), 154–62.

Poland, J. (2003). Helpful tips for writing a thesis, from http://www.hhs.csus.edu/CJ/Word_Docs/Graduate_Handbook_2003ed-Sept03-E-Helpful_Tips_for_Writing_a_Thesis.doc.

Porfeli, E. (2004). *A longitudinal study of a developmental-contextual model of work values during adolescence.* (PhD), The Pennsylvania State University, University Park, PA. Retrieved from http://etda.libraries.psu.edu/theses/approved/WorldWideFiles/ETD-578/porfeli.pdf.

Preiss, K. (2004). The effects of exercise on college students' experience of anxiety. Unpublished MA, Truman State University, Kirksville, MO.

Pringle, A. (1997). A comparison of the cost analysis of three years of special education costs in Danville, Virginia. Unpublished EdD, Virginia Polytechnic Institute and State University, Blacksburg, VA.

Purdue University. (2001). Quoting, paraphrasing, and summarizing. Online Writing Lab. Retrieved on April 24, 2005, from http://owl.english.purdue.edu/handouts/research/r_quotprsum.html.

Ramirez, M. (2007). *Music, gender, and coming of age in the lives of indie rock performers.* (PhD), The University of Georgia, Athens, GA.

Rasmussen, C. (2004). *A community college's culture and its effect on student retention.* (EdD), Wichita State University, Wichita, KS.

Reed, G. (2004). A forgiveness intervention with post-relationship psychologically abused women. Unpublished PhD, University of Wisconsin–Madison, Madison, WI.

Ren, L. (2003). *Imagining China in the era of global consumerism and local consciousness: Media, mobility, and the Spring Festival.* (PhD), Ohio University, Athens, OH. Retrieved from http://www.ohiolink.edu/etd/send-pdf.cgi?acc_num=ohiou1057001670.

Reno, D. (2003). Exploring the process of civic engagement: Phenomenological case study. Unpublished EdD, North Carolina State University, Raleigh, NC.

Revere, D. (2004). Avoiding plagiarism. Retrieved on May 6, 2005, from http://courses.washington.edu/hsstudev/studev/HowToAvoidPlagiarism.htm.

Salem, E. B. (2004). Dissertation proposal writing tutorial: Conceptual framework, from http://www.people.ku.edu/~ebben/tutorial_731.htm.

Shao, X. (2004). *Teacher training and curriculum reform in Chinese agricultural schools.* (PhD), The Pennsylvania State University, University Park, PA. Retrieved from http://etda.libraries.psu.edu/theses/approved/WorldWideFiles/ETD-527/Thesis_Shao.pdf.

Sica, G. (2006). Bias in research studies. *Radiology, 238,* 780–89. Retrieved from http://radiology.rsna.org/content/238/3/780.full doi:10.1148.

Skelton, J., and Edwards, S. (2000). The function of the discussion section in academic medical writing. *British Medical Journal, 320,* 1269–270.

Smith, D. C. (2004). *Substance use attitudes and behaviors of students with learning disabilities.* (PhD), The Ohio State University, Columbus, OH. Retrieved from http://www.ohiolink.edu/etd/send-pdf.cgi?acc_num=osu1092148415.

Strauss, A., and Corbin, J. (1990). *Basics of qualitative research: grounded theory procedures and techniques*. Thousand Oaks, CA: Sage Publications.

Strayer, R. (2010). *Variables predicting success in an advanced medical-surgical nursing course and the NCLEX-RN for pre-licensure baccalaureate nursing students.* (PhD), Temple University.

Suveg, C. (2003). Emotion management in children with anxiety disorders: A focus on the role of emotion-related socialization processes. Unpublished PhD, University of Maine, Orono, ME.

Talbot, A. (2004). *How much information do men really want? Information search behavior and decision rationale in a medical decision-making task for men.* (PhD), The Pennsylvania State University, University Park, PA. Retrieved from http://etda.libraries.psu.edu/theses/approved/WorldWideFiles/ETD-711/AndrewPTalbot_D_11_22_04.pdf.

Taniguchi, S. (2004). *Outdoor education and meaningful learning: Finding the attributes of meaningful learning experience in an outdoor education program.* (Ph.D. Dissertation), Brigham Young University, Salt Lake City, UT.

Taylor, D. (2001). Writing a literature review in the health and social science work, from http://www.utoronto.ca/hswriting/lit-review.htm.

Tellez, F. (2004). *Instrumental use of information in the design of the Chilean Secondary Education Reform.* (PhD), University of Pittsburgh, Pittsburgh, PA.

Thom, C. (2006). *A comparison of the effect of single-sex versus mixed-sex classes on middle school student achievement.* (EdD), Marshall University, Huntington, WV.

Thurman, S. (2004). *The glass ceiling as a mirror: How do women secondary school principals support school improvement?* (EdD), University of Cincinnati, Cincinnati, OH. Retrieved from http://www.ohiolink.edu/etd/send-pdf.cgi?acc_num=ucin1084767759.

Trochim, W. (2006). *Research Methods Knowledge Base.* Mason, OH: Thomas Atomic Dog Publishers.

Uauy, C. (2007). *Positional cloning of gpc-B1, a wheat quantitative trait loci affecting senescence and with pleiotropic effects on grain protein, zinc and iron concentration.* (PhD), University of California, Davis, Davis, CA.

University of Chicago Press. (2010). *The Chicago manual of style* (15th ed.). Chicago, IL: The University of Chicago Press.

University of San Francisco. (2004a). Educating hearts and minds to change the world, October 1, 2006, from http://www.cps.usfca.edu/ob/studenthandbooks/322handbook/coach.htm.

University of San Francisco. (2004b). Format for research proposal. College of Professional Studies. Retrieved on January 20, 2005, from http://www.cps.usfca.edu/ob/resources/format.htm.

University of Wisconsin–Madison Writing Center. (2004). Review of literature, from http://www.wisc.edu/writing/Handbook/ReviewofLiterature.html.

van Teijlingen, E., and Hundley, E. (2001). The importance of pilot studies. *Social Research UpDate, Winter* (35). Retrieved from April 21, 2005 website: http://www.soc.surrey.ac.uk/sru/SRU35.html.

Wabuyele, L. (2003). *Understanding teachers' and administrators' perceptions and experiences towards computer use in Kenyan classrooms: A case study of two schools.* (PhD), Ohio University, Athens, OH. Retrieved from http://www.ohiolink.edu/etd/send-pdf.cgi?ohiou1071169942.

Waddell, C. (2004). *The effects of negotiated written feedback within formative assessment on fourth grade students' motivation and goal orientations.* (PhD), University of Missouri–St. Louis, St. Louis, MO. Retrieved from https://tomsawyer.umsl.edu/webapps/weboffice/ETD/query.cfm?id=f777.

Walonick, D. (2004). Elements of a research proposal and report, from http://www.statpac.com/research-papers/research-proposal.htm-chapter-3.

Walonick, D. (2005). Elements of a research proposal and report. Retrieved May 10, 2012, from http://statpac.org/research-library/research-proposal.htm.

Watson, G. (1997). Beyond the psychological contract: Ideology and the economic social contract in a restructuring environment. Unpublished PhD, Virginia Polytechnic Institute and State University, Blacksburg, VA.

Williams, S. (2004). *A meta-analysis of the effectiveness of distance education in allied health science programs.* (PhD), University of Cincinnati, Cincinnati, OH. Retrieved from http://www.ohiolink.edu/etd/send-pdf.cgi?acc_num=ucin1085017370.

Wong, P. (2002). How to write a research proposal, from http://www.meaning.ca/articles/print/writing_research_proposal_may02.htm.

Workman, L. (2010). *The essential structure of compulsive buying: A phenomenological inqury.* (PhD), Utah State University, Logan, UT.

World Health Organization. (2004). Guidelines for writing a research proposal (protocol). Regional Office for Southeast Asia, Communicable Diseases Department Retrieved May 10, 2012, from http://www.searo.who.int/LinkFiles/CDS_Guideline_Proposal_Development(protocol).pdf.

Yin, R. (2003). Case study research: Design and methods (3rd ed., vol. 5). Thousand Oaks, CA: Sage Publications Inc.

About the Author

Dr. Raymond L. Calabrese is professor of educational administration in the School of Educational Policy and Leadership at The Ohio State University. During his tenure in higher education, he served as faculty and department chair. He has authored or coauthored nine books, two edited books, and over one hundred refereed articles in educational journals. Four of his solely authored books are dedicated to dissertation writing. Dr. Calabrese serves as reviewer for scholarly national and international journals and serves as associate editor of an international education journal. He earned his doctorate at the University of Massachusetts at Amherst. Contact Dr. Calabrese at calabrese.31@osu.edu. Visit his uplifting and positive blog at http://people.ehe.ohio-state.edu/rcalabrese/.